Contemplative Prayer at Work in Our Lives

"*Contemplative Prayer at Work in Our Lives* is a guidebook, and Geoff Colvin is a spiritual cartographer. Drawing on his own experience and longings, Geoff maps the way to our soul; it is not a way that is divorced from our work and relationships, but one that is intertwined with ordinary life. This book is an important resource for anyone seeking a deeper connection with God."

—**TOM STELLA**
Author and co-founder of the
Soul Link Center in Colorado Springs

"Geoff Colvin has captured in one small book the essence of Christian contemplative prayer, asking and answering all the right questions, and making contemplative prayer accessible to the 'everyday Christian.' This will be a popular book not only in established contemplative circles, but in church libraries and religion-based book discussion circles. It is a comprehensive guide for anyone starting out or well on their way on the contemplative spiritual journey."

—**SANDRA JONES WU**
Ministry leader of contemplative prayer,
Episcopal Church of the Resurrection, Eugene, Oregon

"Geoff Colvin has provided a treasure of a book on contemplative prayer. The book is very readable, engaging, practical, and down to earth for guiding Christians to practice contemplative prayer. This is a great resource for personal application and action. It will be helpful to beginners as well as to those very familiar with contemplative prayer."

—**DOROTHY JEAN BEYER, OSB**
Spiritual director and coordinator of Shalom
at the Monastery, Mount Angel, Oregon

"If you are seeking something more than you are finding in prayers and religious services, this is the book for you! Blending stillness and silence, you are invited to create your own 'temple'—to rest in the presence of God. The ineffable is explored with applications for the beginner and the seasoned practitioner from all spiritual traditions. This is a wonderful opportunity to go deeper on your journey!"

—**JERRY BRAZA**
Professor emeritus, meditation teacher,
and author of *Practicing Mindfulness* and *The Seeds of Love*

Contemplative Prayer at Work in Our Lives

Resting in God's Presence and Action

Geoff Colvin

RESOURCE *Publications* • Eugene, Oregon

CONTEMPLATIVE PRAYER AT WORK IN OUR LIVES
Resting in God's Presence and Action

Copyright © 2021 Geoff Colvin. All rights reserved. Except for brief quotations in critical publications or reviews, no part of this book may be reproduced in any manner without prior written permission from the publisher. Write: Permissions, Wipf and Stock Publishers, 199 W. 8th Ave., Suite 3, Eugene, OR 97401.

Resource Publications
An Imprint of Wipf and Stock Publishers
199 W. 8th Ave., Suite 3
Eugene, OR 97401

www.wipfandstock.com

PAPERBACK ISBN: 978-1-6667-0268-2
HARDCOVER ISBN: 978-1-6667-0269-9
EBOOK ISBN: 978-1-6667-0270-5

05/21/21

Scripture quotations are from the New Revised Standard Version Bible, copyright © 1989 the Division of Christian Education of the National Council of the Churches of Christ in the United States of America. Used by permission. All rights reserved.

In loving memory of Karsten Tindal (1990–2018), so deeply missed by his parents Jerry and Linda, his sister Sevrina, and his many devoted friends and relatives.

*If we were to begin in a similar way,
to speak to God with far fewer words and much more heart,
I believe that our heart would have opened up,
and we would have spoken a word of prayer.*[1]

—KARL RAHNER

---

1. Rahner, *Need and the Blessing of Prayer*, 13.

Contents

List of Figures | ix
Preface | xi
Acknowledgments | xvii
Introduction | xix

Section One: Laying the Foundations | 1
   1   Understanding God: Glimpses of the Ineffable | 3
   2   Toward an Understanding of Prayer | 15

Section Two: Erecting the Pillars | 33
   3   The Divine Indwelling | 35
   4   Necessity of Stillness and Silence | 46
   5   Spiritual Pathway: Paved with Detachment | 54

Section Three: Building the Temple | 67
   6   Establishing a Lifelong Practice of Prayer | 69
   7   Contemplative Prayer: Resting in God's Presence | 87
   8   Contemplative Prayer: Consenting to God's Action | 104

      Closing Remarks | 121

      Bibliography | 125

List of Figures

Figure 1: Stages in Building a Temple | xxi
Figure 2: The Various Forms of Prayer | 24

Preface

Discontent is crucial to the emergence of prayer.[1]
—MICHAEL CASEY

"Contemplative prayer" and "at work in our lives" are terms that are not typically associated with the laity. Contemplative prayer is often perceived as a practice reserved for cloistered monks and nuns, hermits, mystics, and retreatants, where silence and distance can be maintained from the busyness of the world. It is typically assumed that this prayer form is not really possible, or practical, for everyday practitioners. This means that prayer practices for these seekers have a different focus, characterized by a somewhat high degree of structure, and usually carried out in groups under the leadership of a priest, such as: liturgies, rituals, readings, sermons, recitations of set prayers, and so on. In more recent times, several spiritual leaders, including Thomas Merton, Thomas Keating, Cynthia Bourgeault, Richard Rohr, Michael Casey, and many others, have provided significant leadership and expertise in bringing the practice of contemplative prayer to everyday practitioners. This book, *Contemplative Prayer at Work in Our Lives*, is my attempt to describe essential elements of contemplative prayer that can be practiced by seekers regardless of how busy they are and how noisy their world is. To make some sense of what I have

1. Casey, *Toward God*, 12.

Preface

written, I need to share a piece of my own spiritual journey on how I gravitated toward the practice of contemplative prayer.

For most of my life I have been a practicing Christian, which means that I attended church regularly from childhood through adulthood, received religious education through my schooling, and was involved with various church practices and activities as an adult. I learned from childhood that prayers, such as the "Hail Mary" or the "Our Father," are something to be *recited*, often times in rote form. I also learned more spontaneous forms of prayer, for example, expressing gratitude to God for the good things that happened during the day, praying for family members and friends in need, and asking for things I need. I received similar instructions and experiences with prayer in my early classes in religious education—essentially, that set prayers are *recited* by rote or expressed in the form of requests for needs and gratitude for positive events. Initially, my prayer experience was totally centered on using words to pray.

In later years, my prayer practice was considerably expanded to include a strong focus on worship, celebration, and community. Religious education classes centered on the church's teachings featuring beliefs, rules for living, and participation in church practices, such as the Mass; ritual ceremonies (weddings, funeral services, and parish events); the Rosary and Stations of the Cross; as well as support services for those in need. These services were generally led by a priest who typically followed established rituals prescribed by the church. Besides the recitation of prayers by the priest and community, the services often included additional activities, such as the singing of hymns with music accompaniment, sermons, processions, readings from Scripture, collections, announcements, and some socializing before and after the service. In addition, these services usually involved a variety of actions or motions—sitting, standing, kneeling, bowing, turning, exchanging peace greetings, and walking in processions. I well recall an uncle of mine, a nonchurch-goer, who was attending a funeral Mass with my family, asking me, "Who starts all the moves?" His takeaway from the service was an experience of constant movement. In

Preface

some cases, although rarely, church services included very short periods of silence, usually following the sermon and after reception of the eucharist. However, the prayer service predominantly consisted of reciting and listening to *words* in different ways, and was accompanied by a range of physical movement.

A little over ten years ago I experienced a strong sense of dryness and discontent with my church practice. I felt as if I was attending and participating because it is what I always did, or what people expected of me, and I knew I'd feel guilty if I did not attend. During the services, I was quite aware I was watching the clock, realizing that I was frequently daydreaming, and feeling relieved when the service was over. I ended up asking myself, "Why am I doing this?" Finding no satisfactory answer, I decided to stop attending the church services and being involved with the church-based activities. At one level, I felt relief by being more honest with myself, but it wasn't that long before I felt an *acute void*. I knew something was missing, yet I didn't feel the need to head back to my church. So, I started to look around. I became interested in churches or gatherings that were markedly different from what I was used to, specifically, ones that were not so busy and were more focused on stillness, silence, and personal or private prayer. During this time, I attended yoga-based gatherings, Quaker, Hindu, and Buddhist services. In effect, I became a *seeker*. In all of this, after approximately one year, I felt strongly drawn to meditation, and in particular to what I experienced at Buddhist services. I then decided to join a Buddhist temple near my home and became more fully engaged with their services and activities for the next four years.

The strongest impact from my time at the Buddhist temple came from the experience of *meditation*—called zazen in Buddhism. It was a totally different experience of prayer to be sitting with other people in a chair, facing the wall for 30–40 minutes in silence and stillness on a regular basis. The day started with zazen and almost all services included a period of zazen. It was very evident that zazen was central to Buddhist teachings and practices at this temple. As Ruth Ozeki, Buddhist author, writes, "in other

Preface

words, no matter where you are, and you return your mind to zazen, it feels like coming home."[2]

The overall experience for me, through this constant exposure to zazen, was the sense of an *inward journey*. I was left alone with my thoughts, feelings, and my own self in stillness and silence—with no *words* or *movement*! This experience was such a contrast to what I was used to with the church-based services that involved constant use of words and movement—an absence of silence or stillness. I began to feel very deeply that this form of meditation was the piece that was missing in my own spiritual journey.

While I felt strongly drawn to the practice of meditation in the Buddhist temple, after a few years, I began to feel an unrest. I was more than comfortable with the notion that meditation was an inward journey, but I could not get around these questions: "A journey to where?" "A journey to what?" In Buddhism, the term "emptiness" is frequently used in response to these questions. The concept of emptiness is very appealing to me at one level, in that it captures the sense of removal of self-interests and delusions that can control our lives. However, I wondered what fills this emptiness—the Buddha nature? The true self?

Meanwhile, I attended a few retreats, and continued with spiritual reading and meditation. It was then that the writings of Trappist monk Thomas Merton (1914–1968), a longtime favorite of mine, fully captured my attention when he wrote:

> At the center of our being is a point of nothingness [Le Point Vierge] which is untouched by sin or illusion . . . This little point of nothingness and of absolute poverty is the pure glory of God in us. It is in everybody.[3]

It was like an "aha" moment for me. Merton answered my question: *It is the divine indwelling that fills this emptiness*. I described this realization to a retreat leader that it seemed ever so much more reassuring to "have a warm spot at my center rather than an emptiness or a void." As I reflected more on Merton's

2. Ozeki, *Tale for the Time Being*, 182.
3. Merton, *Conjectures of a Guilty Bystander*, 158.

Preface

notion of *Le Point Vierge*, and other writings, it became clear to me that I needed a Christocentric approach in my spiritual journey—it was time to go back to my roots. So, I joined a Christian church where meditation, specifically contemplative prayer, is an integral part of their services. My spiritual journey now includes both the *regular church services* AND *meditation* that focuses on silence, stillness, and minimal use words (the piece that was missing).

Another ongoing concern I had was that my meditation practice and church-based services seemed to be separate activities from what I did during the rest of the day. That is, while I believed there should be no separation, I felt I would engage in meditation or participate in church services and then get on with the rest of my day—in reality the activities were separate. However, as my practice of contemplative prayer became more established, I began to realize there are two essential and integral parts to contemplative prayer: first, to rest in the presence of God, and second, to consent to God's action.

It is the second part that addresses the concern I struggled with—where my prayer activities seemed to be separated from my daily living. I began to understand that consenting to God's action refers not only to what may happen during the meditation or at a church service, *but also* what may happen during the rest of the day. This means that contemplative prayer also involves being an agent of God's work in the world. That is, when we consent to God's action, we are committing to being open, receptive, and responsive to God's will throughout the entire day—whenever and wherever we may be called upon. In contemplative prayer, I am slowly learning that my prayer life and daily life should be *seamless*. Moreover, it is becoming clearer to me that resting in the presence of God is not something that is restricted to the meditation period or church services. Rather, it is something that can happen throughout the entire day—at any time and any place. Once again, I have taken to heart words from Thomas Merton: "Meditation has no point and no reality unless it is firmly rooted in *life*."[4] Given the importance of consenting to God's action in contemplative prayer,

---

4. Merton, *Contemplative Prayer*, 39 (emphasis his).

Preface

I have chosen the subtitle of this book as *Resting in God's Presence and Action*.

At this stage, I feel quite blessed in having a reasonable balance between the traditional communal prayer services, *my roots*, and the more private contemplative practice that focuses on an inward journey to my center, where God resides. I sense an unfolding of contemplative prayer into two integral dimensions of resting in the presence of God and consenting to God's action, be it during the meditation period or anytime during the day. However, I know this may change over time as I am quite mindful of some advice I was given during a retreat by the leader Leonard Marcel Roshi, who said to me, "Let your meditation take you where it will."

Acknowledgments

WHILE MY FRIENDS AND colleagues may remark "So you've written a new book," I am well aware that many people have played significant roles in the development and production of *Contemplative Prayer at Work in Our Lives*. It is pleasing to have the opportunity to acknowledge their helpful contributions.

In the first place, I have tried to articulate and share aspects of my personal practice with meditation, specifically contemplation, throughout the book. Consequently, I am especially grateful to Leonard Marcel Roshi, Abbot Ejo McMullen, the late Brother Mark Filut, Father Jeffrey Cooper, and Father Michael Casey. These spiritual leaders have provided immeasurable support in helping me to develop and sustain my contemplative prayer practice through their spiritual direction, writings, teachings, retreats, and personal exchanges.

Most of us find that it is helpful, if not necessary, to have soulmates, *anam cara* friends, or fellow seekers, as we undertake our spiritual pathway. I am very blessed to have a number of kindred souls who have helped and supported me in my journey with contemplative prayer, especially Pat Foley, Jerry Braza, Jim Somers, Mary Sharon Moore, Doug Carnine, Nadine Powell, Bob Wiese, Bill Apel, and Marilyn Nersesian.

I am particularly indebted to Kathleen Horton and Guy Maynard for their insightful feedback to the content and flow of the early drafts of the book. I greatly appreciated their encouragement and gentle urging to expand my own insights and to share more

Acknowledgments

fully my personal experiences with contemplative prayer. They were also particularly helpful in identifying content areas that needed more clarity and development.

It is important to me that this book may be helpful to practitioners in all walks of life. A few people who are active in parish and retreat work reviewed the manuscript with an eye to whether the material was sufficiently grounded and understandable for seekers in general. I am very grateful to Sister Dorothy Jean Beyer, Sandra Wu, Pat Foley, and Susan Turpin for their specific feedback and encouragement from this hands-on perspective.

I am also very grateful to Kylee Lee for her artwork in the book. She has the amazing skill of being able to take ill-formed thoughts and translate them into strong visuals that capture the intended meaning.

Finally, I express my deepest gratitude to my wife Nola and daughter Kylee for the special quality of life that a loving family brings.

Introduction

And the deepest level of communication is not communication, but communion. It is wordless. It is beyond words, and it is beyond speech, and it is beyond concept.[1]

—THOMAS MERTON

CONTEMPLATIVE PRAYER AT WORK in Our Lives: Resting in God's Presence and Action, is written for people who, like me, are seeking *something more* in their own prayer life—something more than reciting prayers and participating in the rituals of church services. In addition, those who are already engaged in meditation in one form or another as part of their spiritual journey may be interested in examining their practice with the hope of enriching their prayer life.

In this book, I focus on just one form of meditation—the practice of *contemplative prayer*. I use this term as a meditation practice that focuses on stillness and silence, with *minimal words*, to rest in God's presence and consent to God's action, not only during the meditation period, but throughout the day.

Essentially, my assumption is that the prayer practices in many Christian churches with a strong emphasis on *words* and ritual *movements*, do not meet the needs of many Christians today. These Christians are looking for something more, not so much to replace the prevailing church practices, but rather for an

---

1. Merton, *Asian Journal of Thomas Merton*, 308.

Introduction

additional piece. Granted, it is evident that many Christians are quite satisfied with current practices in their church, as evidenced by their continued attendance and participation. However, many are not satisfied. We only have to look at the significant decline in church attendance in recent years to see that many have drifted away from church affiliation. Several reasons have been proposed for this trend, such as shifts in cultural values, irrelevance to daily living, outdated teachings, inadequate involvement of laity, and issues with beliefs and faith.

In Western countries, there has been a long-standing interest in the spirituality and practice of prayer in Eastern religions, particularly Buddhism and Hinduism. This movement has often been broadly, and perhaps simply, described loosely as a shift from *religion* to *spirituality*. These "searching" Christians experience a void in their spiritual lives and sense that Eastern spiritual practices may help to fill this void. Much has been written on this subject over the years, such as works by Paul Knitter[2] and Beatrice Bruteau.[3]

It is clear there are many different forms of meditation practiced by Christians, such as centering prayer, contemplative prayer, prayer of the heart, transcendental meditation, *lectio divina*, Ignatian contemplation, guided meditation, and discursive meditation. These various practices of meditation are briefly addressed in chapter 2.

Approximately two years ago, I began a small informal survey with contacts I had come to know from my involvement in retreats and local meditation groups. I had some questions about meditation practices. Specifically, I wanted to know: how they managed and maintained their practice; what difficulties they faced; and which aspects appealed to them. The common threads in the responses, along with my own reflections, were published in a recent article in the Episcopal Café Magazine, titled "Christian Meditation: A Gift from God."[4] While the article was reasonably well received, the most common feedback was that it didn't go

---

2. Knitter, *Without Buddha I Could Not Be a Christian*.
3. Bruteau, *What We Can Learn from the East*.
4. Colvin, "Christian Meditation."

Introduction

far enough. It was clear to me that the respondents were seeking something more in their prayer life and that they were particularly interested in the experiences of stillness and silence afforded in meditation that were not available at their church practices. This book is my attempt to examine these aspects of meditation in more depth, with a particular focus of developing a practice of contemplative prayer for the everyday practitioner.

This book centers on one specific form of meditation, which I am calling *contemplative prayer*, one that has the features of an inward journey, letting go of self, and being practiced in stillness and silence, while intentionally resting in the presence of God and consenting to God's action. Stress is placed on contemplative prayer as a practice that emphasizes the use of *few* or *no words*.

The organization of this book is based on the design of a temple. In the first place, a temple is a particularly fitting metaphor, representing the center of our being as we engage in contemplative prayer. St. Paul reminds us, "Do you not know that your body is a temple of the Holy Spirit within you, which you have from God . . . ?"[5] Secondly, a temple is typically designed and constructed in three stages. First, a foundation is laid, second, pillars are erected, and third, the temple is built (see Figure 1: Stages in Building a Temple).

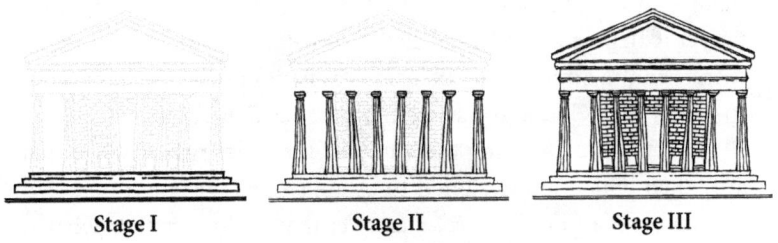

Stage I **Stage II** **Stage III**
Figure 1: Stages in Building a Temple

Regardless of whatever special features the temple may be given, the foundations and pillars need to be firmly in place for the temple to achieve its intended function. In effect, the temple

5. 1 Cor 6:19.

Introduction

requires ongoing support from both the foundations and the pillars, and, conversely, should problems arise with the foundations or the pillars, then the temple itself becomes imperiled. Once the foundations and pillars are in place then the unique features of the temple can be built.

In a similar manner, there are three sections in the design of this book for building and sustaining a contemplative prayer practice based on these stages for constructing a temple. Section 1, "Laying the Foundations," provides essential information on our limited understanding of God and how it relates to our practice of prayer. The assumption is that if these foundational areas are better understood, there is more chance for our contemplative prayer practice to take root in our spiritual journey. In chapter 1, "Understanding God—Glimpses of the Ineffable," questions are raised regarding our limited understanding of God and its impact on our prayer life. Chapter 2, "Toward an Understanding of Prayer," describes some of the common forms of prayer, with a specific focus on contemplation.

Section 2, "Erecting the Pillars," addresses critical underpinnings based on Christian beliefs and practices that support contemplative prayer. Chapter 3, "The Divine Indwelling," describes the fundamental belief that contemplative prayer involves an inward journey to union with God at the center of our being. Chapter 4, "Necessity of Stillness and Silence," emphasizes essential elements—stillness and silence—that set the stage for contemplative prayer. Chapter 5, "Spiritual Pathway—Paved with Detachment," identifies attachments and delusions as major obstacles in our path to union with God and the need to practice detachment.

Section 3, "Building the Temple," identifies typical steps that are taken which are designed to establish and sustain a personal contemplative practice—*your temple*; that is, to examine what it takes to live contemplatively in our spiritual journey. Chapter 6, "Establishing a Lifelong Practice of Prayer," addresses time-tested factors that are important for sustaining a practice—attention to the logistical details of implementation. Chapter 7, "Contemplative Prayer—Resting in God's Presence," describes the first essential element of contemplative prayer as a wordless state of being

Introduction

one with God at the center of our being. Chapter 8, "Contemplative Prayer—Consenting to God's Action" examines the second part of contemplative prayer: how we need to be open, receptive, and ready to follow God's call whenever and wherever the call may come.

Each chapter closes with a section titled "For Personal Application and Action Response." The intent is to provide you with the opportunity to examine aspects of your beliefs and practices related to the content of the chapter that may help to grow your own practice.

For Scripture citations throughout the book, I use the New Revised Standard Version.

Contemplative Prayer at Work in Our Lives includes several meaningful citations from renowned spiritual writers on various aspects of contemplative prayer. The intent is to open gateways to this subject and to help you pursue the topics more fully if you so desire. Also, many of the quotations are drawn from material written in previous centuries before the current standards of inclusive language had been established. No attempt has been made to adjust these writings. While I am aware that noninclusive language may be off-putting, I am reluctant to edit these giants in the field, so I appeal to you to make the mental adjustments as needed.

Contemplative Prayer at Work in Our Lives is designed primarily for seekers who may be looking for ways to revamp their prayer practices, or who feel drawn to a more personal or private form of prayer. My hope is that the content of this book may open a door for these seekers and offer some helpful direction and food for thought in their spiritual journey.

The book may also serve as a useful resource to professionals and those who are experienced in the ways of contemplative prayer and who are in a position of supporting others in their journey. These support personnel include clergy, spiritual directors, sponsors, mentors, counselors, and those who have established meditation practices. In addition, the book may also be useful to those involved in churches and organizations with adult education and parish renewal programs.

Section One

Laying the Foundations

THE PURPOSE OF THIS first section is to address some essential background information on prayer designed to provide a broader context for understanding contemplative prayer. Given the intent of prayer is to grow our union with God, it is helpful to examine how we view God—to the extent it is possible (chapter 1). In addition, given there is full array of prayer services and practices available, by examining these various prayer forms we may be in a better position to understand the unique features of contemplative prayer (chapter 2). The overall assumption is that by addressing our understanding of God and the various forms of prayer, there will be more chances for our practice of contemplative prayer to take root as an integral part of our spiritual journey.

1

Understanding God
Glimpses of the Ineffable

But if a man lies in wait until he does catch the taste of the divine, ever afterward he is a glad seeker of God.[1]

—MEISTER ECKHART

THE PRACTICE OF MEANINGFUL prayer lies at the heart of this book. Karl Rahner, German Jesuit priest and theologian, in writing on prayer with profound simplicity, said, "In prayer we open our hearts to God."[2] While there are a variety of ways to open our hearts in prayer, the focus of prayer is God—the One to whom we are praying. This implies that we must have some understanding and beliefs about God in order to pray in the first place. Moreover, our understanding of God will, presumably, dictate *how we pray*—whether it be "to God," or "with God," or "in God."

It may seem strange, perhaps pointless, to open a book with a chapter on our understanding of God when there is no way we can rightly or fully understand God. However, this does not mean

---

1. Eckhart, *Pocket Meister Eckhart*, 3.
2. Rahner, *Need and the Blessing of Prayer*, 3.

we cannot have *some* understanding of God, nor does it mean God has revealed nothing of the divinity to us. Rather, we have been given what we might call *glimpses* of God.

I am reminded of an exchange in a physics class during my studies at the University of Sydney in the 60s. A student asked the professor, Harry Messell, a leading atomic physicist in Australia at the time, "What do you think of when you think of an electron?" This was a loaded question because an electron has properties of both a particle and a wave—two independent or mutually exclusive physical entities. He answered quite quickly, "A mathematical equation." His message to us was that he doesn't have an image or concept to capture the totality of the properties of an electron. He went on to say, "And if you ask me that question in ten years' time, I will have a different answer."

I learned two things from that exchange: First, we don't have the words to adequately describe certain instances in our universe, and second, what we do understand will change over time as additional research and information come into play. While this illustration belongs to the natural order of science, I see similar limitations in trying to find words, concepts, or images to capture the fullness of God, and the limited understanding we have presently will likely change over time.

In this chapter I try to address the subject of what we can understand about God, realizing the inherent limitations and how this understanding impacts our prayer life and spiritual journey. Topics to be examined are: 1) Our evolving understanding of God, 2) only grace enables authentic understanding of God, and 3) living with the unknown.

Our Evolving Understanding of God

Given the experience of prayer is a very personal and individual matter, it follows that our understanding of God will vary from individual to individual. However, there are some commonalities that may be helpful to address as we examine our own understanding of God in our spiritual path. One way to describe these commonalities is to view them as two distinct phases: from childhood to adulthood, and from rational to spiritual.

Childhood to Adulthood

Many of us who were introduced to prayer as children grew up thinking of God as some kind of supreme being "out there" who created us and the world we live in. We learned that God was the ultimate *father figure* who took care of us. We also learned that God lived in heaven and that, if we did the right thing in life, then one day we would spend forever in heaven with God. We saw God as a person and our prayers centered on speaking to God, person to person, with words centered on themes of gratitude, requests, sorrow for wrong-doing, and love (as in loving another person such as a parent). This means that we were introduced at an early age to an understanding of God as a *supernatural being*—a being *beyond* beings.

While this understanding of God as a benevolent father watching over us worked for us as children, many of us began to find that adult experiences did not mesh with this childhood image of God. For example, as adults we became more aware of the awesome beauty in nature, such as in vast canyons, waterfalls, and sunsets. We also began to sense a presence of the divine in certain acts of kindness, compassion, heroism, and forgiveness by people. In effect, we sensed a presence of God displayed in human virtues and in nature right here, right now, in the world we live in. This sense could not be explained by an exclusive supernatural God, a God somewhere out there. Tom Stella, retreat leader and author, highlighted the inadequacy of our typical understanding of God from our upbringing in relation to our many experiences as adults when he wrote:

> A theistic understanding of God (one that imagines God to be a distant and demanding Supreme Being) is deeply embedded in our hearts as well as in our minds.... Despite their lingering presence, these stereotype notions of God are no longer viable for many who seek to live in the

Section One: Laying the Foundations

to the spiritual dimension they sense in themselves and in all creation.[3]

Consequently, our adult understanding of God needs to accommodate the sense of God's *immanence*. Teachings abound on the subject of the immanent presence of God in Scripture. For example: "And the earth shone with his glory,"[4] "The heavens are telling the glory of God,"[5] and "The kingdom of heaven is now near."[6]

Similarly, spiritual writers consistently teach that God is present to us in so many ways both in the world and within ourselves. For example, Gerard Manley Hopkins, famed poet, writes:

> The world is charged with the grandeur of God.
> It will flame out, like shining from shook foil . . .[7]

In a similar vein, Thomas Keating, author and founder of Centering Prayer, writes: "The spiritual journey does not require going anywhere because God is already present and within us."[8] In addition he notes that, "The chief thing that separates us from God is the thought that we are separated from Him."[9]

The challenge then, as seekers, is to come up with images or thoughts that capture our evolving understanding of God as both *transcendent* and *immanent*. As Dietrich Bonhoeffer, a German pastor and theologian who was imprisoned and executed during World War II for alleged anti-Nazi activities, beautifully says in so few words: "God is the beyond in our midst."[10]

Paul Knitter, author and theologian, explains that our understanding of God has been limited by *dualism,* in that we have emphasized our separation from God, thereby limiting our understanding of God and subsequently our spiritual practices. He goes

---

3. Stella, *God Instinct,* 20.
4. Ezek 43:2.
5. Ps 19:1.
6. Matt 3:2.
7. Hopkins, "God's Grandeur," 66.
8 Keating, *Open Mind, Open Heart,* 20.
9 Keating, *Open Mind, Open Heart,* 33.
10. Bonhoeffer, *Letters and Papers from Prison,* 282.

Understanding God

on to say we need *nondualistic* language, stressing the *interbeing* nature of God:

> Thinking about or imaging God as Interbeing and relating to God as the connecting Spirit is a major antidote to the dualism that has infected Christian theology and spirituality. . . . Therefore, a better image for creation might be a pouring forth of God, an extension of God, in which the Divine carries on the divine activity of interrelating *in* and *with* and *through* creation.[11]

Similarly, Marcus Borg, late Professor of Religion at Oregon State University, uses the term *panentheism*, which affirms both transcendence (God's otherness or moreness) and immanence (God's presence within us).[12] He goes on to explain:

> In the absence of an obvious choice, I suggest "Spirit" as a root image for this model of God [panentheism] . . . It leads to an image of the Christian life that stresses relationship, intimacy, and belonging.[13]

It is clear for many of us, as we travel along our spiritual path, that we keep trying to unravel the mystery of God in a way that enriches or deepens our journey. We also become more aware that such an understanding of God is beyond our intellect. So, while we may advance our appreciation of God, we also recognize that our knowledge of God falls way short of the fullness of God's reality. We also have found that what we think we know about God can limit or even impede our understanding of the true God. In fact, we may need to follow the advice of Karen Armstrong, Professor of Comparative Religions:

> One of the conditions of enlightenment has always been a willingness to let go of what we thought we knew in order to appreciate truths we had never dreamed of.[14]

---

11. Knitter, *Without Buddha I Could Not Be a Christian*, 21–22 (emphasis original).
12. Borg, *God We Never Knew*, 32.
13. Borg, *God We Never Knew*, 71.
14. Armstrong, *Case for God*, xviii.

Section One: Laying the Foundations

At the close of this section, I wish to briefly describe my own evolving understanding of God and the various forms of prayer. As a child and young adult, I saw God as the supernatural being "out there." My prayers were essentially centered on words, both vocal and subvocal. Around middle age, I became more aware of God as immanent, present to us in the world and with people. My prayers became more celebratory of life, nature, and events, with gratitude as a constant theme. Toward retirement, I found myself responding to God within, at the very center of my being. My prayer life focused more on meditation, trying to let go of thoughts, distractions, and emotions, and to respond more fully to God's presence within and consent to God's action. Today I see another shift that I can best describe through this exchange I had recently with a friend:

Friend:	What is your concept of God?
Me:	God.
Friend:	Yes, well what do you think of when you hear the word God?
Me:	God.
Friend:	You are not answering my question.
Me:	If I added more words I would not be speaking of God.

In this sense I don't feel the need to come up with words to describe my understanding of God, realizing that by so doing I am limiting God and end up with less understanding, or mistaken understanding. My preferred focus in prayer now is best described as trying to rest in the presence and action of God without words—be it within me, in nature, in others, or in life. This is not to say I have abandoned other forms of prayer or graduated from them. On the contrary, I still use many of them at different times, but have now *added* a new prayer form—contemplative prayer.

Only Grace Enables Authentic Understanding of God

A fundamental Christian belief is that our true understanding of God is totally predicated on it being a gift from God—a *grace*. Sure, we can read, reflect, philosophize, and draw on logic, science, and theology to explore notions of God. However, in this way we are limited to what might be called human descriptions of God. As Tom Stella aptly writes, "It is natural to make 'Him' into our own image and likeness."[15] However, to understand God as God is, the bottom line is that any such authentic understanding has to be attributed to the grace of God. Spiritual writers have, through the centuries, been very clear on this fundamental belief that grace, God's gift to us, is at the heart of our spiritual path. For example, the Anonymous Author of *The Cloud of Unknowing*, in a classic work on Christian Mysticism from the fourteenth century, writes:

> Yet for all this, when God's grace arouses you to enthusiasm, it becomes the lightest sort of work there is and one most willingly done. Without his grace, however, it is very difficult, and almost, I should say, quite beyond you.[16]

Similarly, in recent times, Michael Casey, Trappist monk and international retreat leader, explains:

> The benevolence of God expresses itself in so many different ways as our journey unfolds. Gradually we come to realize that everything that happens in our life is somehow the gift of our loving Father . . . So, the point that I want to emphasize is that the most important happenings on our spiritual journey are not the result of our own actions but are gifts of God . . .[17]

The practicing Christian may very well ask, "What does it look like to have God's grace acting in our lives?" Clearly, the experience of God's grace will vary from person to person. St. John

---

15. Stella, *God Instinct*, 21.

16. Anonymous Author, *Cloud of Unknowing & The Book of Privy Counseling*, 40.

17. Casey, *Grace*, vii–ix.

Section One: Laying the Foundations

the apostle teaches us, "No one can come to me unless drawn by the Father who sent me."[18] A key word in this message for describing the action of grace is *drawn*. That is, the individual experiences a sense of becoming aware of, and attracted to, doing something or receiving something. This experience is stronger than curiosity. Rather, it is better described as a *tug*. In my own case, for example, several years ago I felt my prayer practice at church services had dried up (as I mentioned in the preface). I stopped going to church, and I remember very clearly being *drawn to meditation*. I checked out the meditation services at various churches and centers. I ended up joining a Buddhist temple where I was able to practice meditation quite extensively. After nearly four years I sensed an emptiness that was unsettling. I needed something at my center—maybe a Christ-centered approach. This movement felt like I was being *drawn* to making a return to a Christian church. I found a church where meditation is practiced as an integral part of the available services, and where, I am grateful to say, I feel very much at home. I believe that God's grace, revealing itself in the sense of being drawn to meditation first, and then a return to a particular Christian church, has been a blessing for me in my spiritual journey.

I shared this experience of feeling drawn to meditation with a friend who has a regular meditation practice. His comment was that he didn't feel drawn so much as he felt there was something within that was *alive*. When he meditated, he sensed he was keeping it alive. In each of our cases, we believed God's grace was present and active in gifting us with a desire to establish and sustain a meditation practice.

Living with the Unknown

Since earliest times, Christians have been taught that to gain some understanding of God, a glimpse of God, we need to let go of our

---

18. John 6:44.

Understanding God

own thoughts and images and allow the grace of God to operate. For example, the Anonymous Author writes:

> It doesn't matter how much profound wisdom we possess about created spiritual beings; our understanding cannot help us gain knowledge about any uncreated spiritual being, who is God alone. But the failure of our understanding can help us. When we reach the end of what we know, that's where we find God. That's why Dionysius said that the best, most divine knowledge of God is that which is known by not-knowing.[19]

Unfortunately, we possess a powerful disposition to take charge and acquire complete answers to our questions. The very idea of waiting for God's truth to be revealed just partially and unpredictably becomes a daunting challenge. Our new role becomes one of being open, receptive, and responsive to the action of God's grace, however and whenever it may arise. One major issue is that when we are able to let go of our preformed thoughts or images of God and learn to live with the unknown, we are left with a void. We simply don't like voids. However, it is in this very void, where we put our *trust* in God, that we prepare ourselves to receive God's grace. Simone Weil, the twentieth-century French philosopher, activist, and mystic, reminds us:

> Grace fills empty spaces, but it can only enter where there is a void to receive it, and it is grace itself which makes this void.[20]

In addition to the demands involved with loss of control when we let go of our preconceived notions of God and trust in God's grace, is the experience of *waiting*. We simply put ourselves in a position of being open and receptive to whatever and whenever God's grace may be revealed to us. Essentially, we are in *a waiting game*. The problem is that waiting has become anathema, a curse, in today's culture. Modern technology has trained us well

---

19. Anonymous Author, *Cloud of Unknowing with the Book of Privy Counsel*, 156.
20. Weil, *Love in the Void*, 75.

Section One: Laying the Foundations

to expect things to be done quickly and with minimal wait times. Consequently, when we have to wait, even for minutes longer than expected, we become agitated. It is in this cultural context of very low tolerance, aversion in fact, for waiting that we are invited to wait for God's grace to be revealed in our spiritual pathway. Two suggestions are offered based on a Christian approach to help us better deal with waiting as an integral part of our prayer practice.

The first suggestion is to seize the moments where waiting occurs in our daily lives as *opportunities* for prayer. A friend once commented to me that once she developed a regular practice of meditation, she found that there was little to no wait time during her day. Essentially, she used the wait times that occurred during the day as moments for prayer. Other wait times that regularly occur include when we are: stopped at a light, parked in the pick-up line at school, waiting in line at the store, on hold for a phone call, waiting at the coffee shop for a friend, watching the kettle boil, and so on. A common feature in these examples of wait time is that the wait time will be ended and the *expected result will occur,* such as the lights will turn green, the friend will show up, and we will get to the front of the line to be served. A useful Christian practice during these moments is to recite a short prayer, perhaps connected to Scripture, accepting the wait and putting ourselves in God's presence. For example: I wish to, "Be still before the Lord, and wait patiently for him."[21]

A second situation involving wait time that is more challenging is the occasion when the wait time is *open-ended* in that we do not know the results. For example, when we apply for a job, we do not know the outcome, or when we have surgery, a host of outcomes are possible. While we may wish for a particular outcome, and do what we can to achieve it, the results are still indeterminate. Priest and renowned spiritual leader Henri Nouwen describes for us a valuable approach to help us raise these open-ended waiting times to prayerful opportunities. He mentions two phases in Jesus' life as *before* and *after* he was "handed over"[22] following his arrest.

---

21. Ps 37:7.
22. Nouwen, *Path of Waiting,* 33.

Understanding God

The first phase consists of his active life where he initiated a variety of activities—preaching, teaching, traveling, healing, working miracles, and transforming the lives of his disciples. The second phase, after Jesus was handed over, marks when Jesus was subject to the call of others—led to the high priest, taken to Pilate, tried by the Jewish council, crowned with thorns, and crucified. Nouwen goes on to say if we wish to follow Jesus, there needs to be the same two phases in our journey—one where we control the initiatives and the other where we are not in control. It is the latter part that directly applies to waiting on God's grace in an open-ended way, not knowing when or where we may be led. Our waiting in this open-ended way not only applies to God's grace in our understanding of God, but in the many steps of our spiritual pathway.

Nouwen also teaches us that while we wait for God's action that God is also waiting for our response. There is essentially an *ongoing reciprocal waiting*—God waits for our response and we wait for God's action, as Nouwen concludes:

> Imagine how important that message is for people in our world. If it is true that God in Jesus is waiting for our response to divine love, then we can discover a whole new perspective on how to wait in life . . . It is also participating in God's own waiting for us and in that way coming to share in the deepest purity of love, which is God's love.[23]

In sum, we have been given glimpses of the divine. This means we have been graced with some understanding of God that draws us into God's presence and encourages us to more fully commit to our spiritual path.

For Personal Application

1. If you were asked to describe God, what words would come to you?

---

23. Nouwen, *Path of Waiting*, 45–46.

Section One: Laying the Foundations

2. How did you view God when you were a child?
3. Has this view changed as an adult?
4. Do you see your understanding of God as a gift from God?
5. How do you rate yourself concerning your ability to live with the unknown?
6. How do you manage wait time?

> **Action Response**: Is there something *specific* in this chapter that draws you to make a change in, or to add to, your spiritual journey?

2

Toward an Understanding of Prayer

O most merciful Redeemer, Friend and Brother,
May I know Thee more clearly,
Love Thee more dearly,
And follow Thee more nearly.[1]

—ST. RICHARD OF CHICHESTER

WE CAN EXPECT THAT Christians would agree that the practice of prayer is an integral and essential part of our spiritual journey. It seems impossible to conceive the undertaking of union with God without a deep commitment to prayer. However, we see considerable variability, as well as uncertainty, when it comes down to understanding what prayer is and how we pray. For example, if we asked Christians what prayer means to them, or how they practice prayer, we would get a wide array of responses such as that prayer is: conversing with God, communing with God, doing God's will, participating in church services, being aware of God's presence in all things, helping a neighbor in need, taking a relaxing walk along a path near a river, reciting the Rosary, chanting the Psalms,

---

1. St. Richard of Chichester, "Acts and Other Devotions," 31.

Section One: Laying the Foundations

withdrawing to a quiet place to sit in God's presence, petitioning God for some need, and so on. Each of these activities represents a familiar and traditional Christian practice of prayer. While a considerable variety of prayer forms are available, Christians are still challenged when it comes to sustaining a regular prayer practice. One reason is that the prayer rituals with standardized words, actions, and roles become too much of a routine, leading to a troubling dullness for some Christians (as noted in my own case in the preface). There is a need to engage in forms of prayer that are more private, more personal, and rely less on words, actions, and rituals (a theme of this book). Another reason is our understanding of prayer is perhaps too limited and somewhat misplaced. Granted, we are dealing with a mystery in trying to understand prayer, and the same goes for trying to understand God (addressed in the previous chapter). However, we can still learn more and understand more about prayer that will likely enhance and enrich our prayer life while accepting that we will never attain full understanding.

The purpose of this chapter is to try to deepen our understanding of prayer with a focus on one particular prayer form—contemplative prayer. The topic areas include: 1) Understanding that prayer is a gift from God, 2) prayer as a personal practice, 3) clarification of our role in prayer, 4) the range of prayer forms, 5) forms of meditation, 6) contemplative prayer, and 7) reviewing one's practice.

Understanding That Prayer Is a Gift from God

A central belief in the Christian tradition is that prayer is intrinsically and fundamentally a *gift* from God. Unfortunately, many practitioners operate as though sheer effort, along with fervent searches for methods of prayer, can make prayer simply happen, or at least contribute to making it happen. Over the past few years, I have had the opportunity to help lead and participate in retreats and prayer services. The theme that prayer is a *gift from God* seems to be puzzling to many of the participants who have shared comments like:

Toward an Understanding of Prayer

- I was never taught that when I was growing up.
- Makes me wonder why I work so hard at prayer.
- I guess I believe that prayer is a gift from God, but you wouldn't know it by the way I try to pray.
- If you attended our Sunday service, you would come away thinking that it is the priest and the congregation that make prayer happen.
- If I really believe this, I would pray differently. I would be much more laid back and would show more gratitude in my prayers.
- I, and I think many others, were brought up with prayer practices that were all about us talking to and making requests from God without any expectation that God might want to talk to us.

For me personally, the belief that prayer is a gift from God—and its implications—has had the biggest impact on my own practice. As I learn to accept that prayer is a gift, I have taken a more effortless approach by trying to rest in the presence of God and to be responsive to God's action. Believing that prayer is a gift from God frees me to assume a much more passive and receptive mode. Rather than focusing so much on technique or formula, I can put my energy into being receptive and responsive to this gift and to trust where it may take me.

To better understand that prayer is a gift from God, it may be helpful to reflect on some spiritual readings. For example, both the Old and New Testaments, along with the writings from spiritual leaders, provide us with constant reminders that it is God's grace and limitless gifts acting in us and transforming us that are the bases of authentic prayer.

Section One: Laying the Foundations

Scripture

Likewise, the Spirit helps us in our weakness; for we do not know how to pray as we ought, but that very Spirit intercedes with sighs too deep for words.[2]

For by grace you have been saved through faith, and this is not your own doing; it is the gift of God—not the result of works, so that no one may boast. For we are what he has made us, created in Christ Jesus for good work, which God prepared beforehand to be our way of life.[3]

May you be made strong with all the strength that comes from his glorious power, and may you be prepared to endure everything with patience, while joyfully giving thanks to the Father, who has enabled you to share in the inheritance of the saints in the lights.[4]

For it is God who is at work in you, enabling you both to will and to work for his good pleasure.[5]

Grace is poured upon your lips. Therefore, God has blessed you forever.[6]

By the grace of God I am what I am.[7]

If you knew the gift of God, and who it is that is saying to you, "Give me a drink," you would have asked him, and he would have given you living water.[8]

---

2. Rom 8:26.
3. Eph 2:8–10.
4. Col 1:11–13.
5. Phil 1:13.
6. Ps 45:2.
7. 1 Cor 15:10.
8. John 4:10.

Spiritual Writings

Meister Eckhart

But if a man seeks God's will alone, whatever flows from that or is revealed by that, he may take as a gift from God without ever looking or considering whether it is my nature or grace or whence it comes or in what wise; he need not care about that.[9]

Michael Casey

Contemplation is entirely gratuitous, pure grace: on God's part, total gift; on ours, total receptivity.[10]

Thomas Merton

True contemplation is not a psychological trick but a theological grace. It can come to us only as a gift, and not a result of our own clever use of spiritual techniques.[11]

Cynthia Bourgeault

The mercy of God does not come and go, granted to some and refused to others. Why? Because it is unconditional—always there, underlying everything. It is literally the force that holds everything in existence, the gravitational field in which "we live and move and have our being" (Acts 17:28). Mercy is God's innermost being

---

9. Eckhart, *Complete Mystical Works of Meister Eckhart*, 290.
10. Casey, *Grace*, 122.
11. Merton, *Climate of Monastic Prayer*, 115–16.

Section One: Laying the Foundations

turned outward to sustain the visible and created world in unbreakable love.[12]

These readings from Scripture, spiritual writers, and so many others not mentioned, are incredibly rich in explaining to us that our whole purpose in creation is union with God and that it is God's grace that makes this possible. It is important, as we examine our prayer life, that we take time to quietly reflect on these or related readings. In this way, we may become more aware of, grateful for, and responsive to the boundless manifestations of God's gifts in our lives.

Prayer as a Personal Practice

No one would suggest that there is only one way to exercise our bodies or to take care of our physical well-being. There is no "one size fits all." We understand our bodies are quite unique in so many ways so that one form of exercise can be beneficial to one person, harmful to another, or not practical for someone else. Consequently, in most communities we will find an extensive variety of options for keeping fit and healthy. In addition, there are several ways to exercise at home or simply by yourself. It all comes down to what works best for you. If you wish to establish and sustain a regular exercise practice, a desirable goal for everyone, the imperative is to find ways of exercising that fit in with your schedule and with the way you like to exercise.

The same can be said of prayer, especially the practice of meditation. We are different in so many ways, such as in our unique relationship with God, the distinct individuality in our physical and mental make-up, available time, employment demands, personal and family needs, and so on. This individual variability will impact the way we pray. As with physical exercise, there is no one-size-fits-all method. The guiding rule for establishing and sustaining a regular prayer practice is to find what works best for you given your unique needs. It is typically recommended that you immerse

---

12. Bourgeault, *Mystical Hope*, 25.

Toward an Understanding of Prayer

yourself in the prayer forms that you may feel drawn to and see what feels comfortable or what seems to be a good fit for yourself.

Clarification of Our Role in Prayer

Just as with any commitment, it is critical to understand your own particular role—to be aware of what you can or should do as well as what you should avoid. The same is true for developing and sustaining a personal practice of prayer—you need to understand what is involved with any particular prayer form, such as: the limitations of certain practices, beliefs underlying the practice, and knowing what efforts and actions are helpful in growing the prayer practice.

Futility of Misdirected Efforts

Much as we may believe that all prayer is a gift from God, we often delude ourselves into thinking our efforts and search for methods can make prayer happen for us. We only have to look at the multiplicity of books, online programs, apps, and YouTube clips that are readily available to help us to pray effectively. While these aids may be helpful, we need to constantly assess whether we think we are the ones who facilitate prayer—that by following these methods and exercising effort, we will attain fuller union with God. Thomas Merton often wrote on this misconception or delusion:

> The only trouble is that in the spiritual life there are no tricks and no shortcuts. Those who imagine that they can discover spiritual gimmicks and put them to work for themselves usually ignore God's will and his grace.[13]

Merton goes on to point out that one of the big hazards in thinking we can control the results of prayer is that we become discouraged when our expectations do not occur. We then may abandon prayer or become trapped in futile efforts. Merton writes:

13. Merton, *Contemplative Prayer*, 37.

Section One: Laying the Foundations

> People who try to pray and meditate above their proper level, who are too eager to reach what they believe to be a "high degree of prayer," get away from the truth and from reality. In observing themselves and trying to convince themselves of their advance, they become imprisoned in themselves. Then they realize that grace has left them, they are caught in their own emptiness and futility and remain helpless.[14]

It is most important as we try to develop our prayer life that we avoid the trap of attending too much to our own efforts and expectations. Rather, we must learn to realize that prayer is a gift from God and to pray accordingly.

Our Role in Prayer

Given we need to be very mindful that our own efforts in developing a prayer practice can lead us astray, we need to humbly ask, "What then is our role in developing a prayer practice?" The answer to this question lies in *how our efforts are directed*. Rather than directing our efforts toward our own ends or expectations, we need to focus on becoming *ready* to receive God's grace—to be *receptive, open, trusting,* and *responsive* to the presence of God, and to consent to God's action. This message is very clear in St. Paul's teachings:

> Likewise, the Spirit helps us in our weakness; for we do not know how to pray as we ought, but that very Spirit intercedes with sighs too deep for words.[15]

Our role becomes one of putting our effort and energy into a twofold readiness: 1) Being ready to rest in God's presence, which involves waiting, gazing, and being still without words in silence, and 2) being ready to consent to God's action as it may be revealed to us. Henri Nouwen, in reflecting on his own prayer practice, shared that he needed to become a "little useless" to allow God's action in authentic prayer:

---

14. Merton, *Contemplative Prayer*, 37.
15. Rom 8:26.

Toward an Understanding of Prayer

> Thinking about my own prayer, I realize how easily I make it into a little seminar with God, during which I want to be useful by reading beautiful prayers, thinking profound thoughts, and saying impressive words. I am obviously still worried about the grade! It indeed is a hard discipline to be useless in God's presence and to let him speak in the silence of my heart. But whenever I become a little useless, I know that God is calling me to a new life beyond the boundaries of my usefulness.[16]

It is also important to understand that God's gift of prayer is an open-ended benevolence. Thomas Merton teaches that the more open and responsive we become, the more likely we may experience God's grace on our spiritual journey:

> If the life of prayer is to transform our spirit . . . then prayer must be accompanied by "conversion," *metanoia*, that deep change of heart in which we die on a certain level of our being in order to find ourselves alive and free on another, more spiritual level.[17]

In effect, authentic prayer is fundamentally a gift from God, and our role is one of being ready, open, receptive, and responsive. In addition, this gift keeps on giving as we journey on our spiritual path. L. J. Milone, director of faith formation at St. John the Baptist Catholic Church in Silver Spring, Maryland, summarizes this theme very succinctly when he writes, "Divine grace starts, sustains, and ends the journey."[18]

The Range of Prayer Forms

There is no question that there are many ways to pray that give rise to a full array of prayer forms. For example, there are several regularly scheduled church-based services designed to help Christians pray together, such as: the Mass and Eucharist, which involve

---

16. Nouwen, "Let Yourself Be Useless," para. 2.
17. Merton, *Climate of Monastic Prayer*, 84.
18. Milone, *Nothing but God*, 11.

recitation of prayers, singing, chanting, reflection on Scripture, and reception of the Eucharist; services related to the sacraments; celebrations marking certain times during the church's liturgical cycle; and so on. Then there are the more private, personal, and silent prayer forms of meditation (the focus of this book). Sometimes it can be confusing to understand how these various prayer forms work together or are different.

Figure 2: The Various Forms of Prayer shows the interface between prayer, meditation, and contemplative prayer. The largest, or outside circle, represents the universe of prayer, that is, all forms of prayer comprised of church-based services and small group and individual prayer practices, such as various forms of meditation that include contemplation. The next circle, meditation, falls inside the prayer circle, denoting that it is an example of prayer forms. The smallest circle, contemplative prayer, lies within the meditation circle, indicating that it is an example of meditation and belongs to the prayer form of meditation, all of which are forms of prayer.

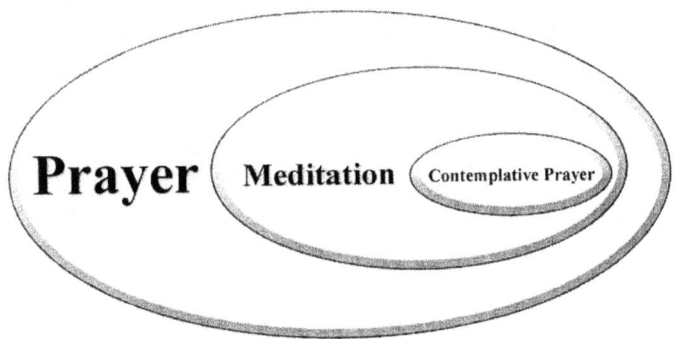

Figure 2: The Various Forms of Prayer

Forms of Meditation

Meditation, by different names, underpinnings of beliefs, and formats, is a central practice in all of the world's major religions,

Toward an Understanding of Prayer

including: Buddhism, Islam, Judaism, Hinduism, and Christianity. For the purposes of this book, the focus is Christian approaches to meditation, specifically contemplative prayer, that share the common features of: letting go of self; maintaining stillness and silence; journeying within to one's center where God resides, while intentionally seeking the presence and union with God. Christians who practice meditation typically have the opportunity to meditate regularly as part of a group, or privately at home, or in other settings. Many report that they engage in *both* individual and group meditation, and that this combination serves to enrich and sustain their overall practice. In addition, longer opportunities for meditation are frequently available in the form of retreats held at churches and retreat centers.

The practice of meditation has often been likened to climbing a mountain. In making a climb there are several options for routes, equipment, and techniques. However, there is just the one desired outcome—the experience of reaching and resting at the top of the mountain. The same is true for meditation. There are several approaches or methods in meditation, but they all have the one intention—union with God. Some of the more common forms of meditation in Christian practices include: guided meditation, Ignatian contemplation, prayer of the heart, transcendental meditation, discursive meditation, centering prayer, and contemplative prayer. A brief description of these forms of meditation is provided to apprise you of what is available and to help sharpen the distinctive features of the focus of this book—contemplative prayer. At the risk of oversimplifying these different approaches to meditation, I have included a resource that should provide more in-depth descriptions, and I encourage you to read more about these approaches as needed.

Guided Meditation

As the name suggests, guided meditation is a process by which one or more participants practice meditation in response to the step-by-step direction provided by a trained practitioner or teacher, either in person, online, or by means of text, recordings, or apps. Typically, music and instruction are interspersed during the meditation period. This method is very helpful to those who are somewhat new to meditation, or who prefer more structure to help maintain attention, and for those who may be enduring pain and discomfort.

Resource: Eckhart Tolle.[19]

Ignation Contemplation

This centuries-old meditation form was developed by St. Ignatius of Loyola in the 1500s to help Christians come to know and follow Jesus through direct interaction with Scripture. The approach is to help fully enter the Scripture story with all of our intellect, senses, and imagination as we slowly and prayerfully read a selected passage. The idea is that we become a participant in the story, and that we continue the story in our heart and mind, following the scriptural reading. Emphasis is placed on letting the Spirit guide the prayer.

Resource: Timothy Gallagher.[20]

Discursive Meditation

This approach to meditation is thinking-oriented so that the mind and imagination are actively engaged in trying to understand and apply sacred Scripture and spiritual writings. Essentially, it is a reasoned application by the mind of some spiritual truth with the intent of penetrating its meaning, and, with God's grace, then carrying it into practice. The deep reflection on Scripture helps us to let go of our own thoughts and feelings to enter periods or states of internal silence. This approach is often referred to as *lectio divina*.

Resource: Christine Valters Paintner.[21]

---

19. Tolle, *Essential Meditations with Eckhart Tolle*.
20. Gallagher, *Meditation and Contemplation*.
21. Paintner, *Lectio Divina*.

Toward an Understanding of Prayer

Prayer of the Heart

This form of prayer has been widely practiced for centuries in Eastern religions, especially in Islam and Hinduism, and emphasizes sustained repetition of certain phrases—a mantra. A Christian counterpart from these early times also involves an emphasis on the unceasing repetition of the Jesus Prayer: "Lord Jesus Christ, Son of God, have mercy on me, a sinner." The late Fr. John Main has been instrumental in establishing this form meditation practice in the West.

Resource: John Main.[22]

Transcendental Meditation™

This form of meditation, of Hindu origin, was introduced by Maharishi Mahesh Yogi to the West in the 1950s. The expression "transcendental" has its roots in the word *trans-*, meaning crossing the barriers between the physical and spiritual, and *transcending*, indicating a surpassing of normal experiences. This meditation form has been widely adopted by Hindus and other religions, including Christianity, and is widely used in medical and other professional fields to help participants relax and clear their minds. The chanting of a mantra is commonly used.

Resource: Jack Forem.[23]

Important Note: Each of these examples of meditation forms involves the use of words or symbols to engage our intellect, mind, senses, emotions, or imagination. By using our faculties, our attention is focused on some object as an integral step in the meditation process. By contrast, as we will see in the remaining chapters, contemplative prayer is designed to diminish the role of our faculties and allow our attention to rest solely in the presence and action of God.

---

22. Main, *Words into Silence*.
23. Forem, *Transcendental Meditation*.

Section One: Laying the Foundations

Contemplative Prayer

First and foremost, contemplative prayer shares these common features with all forms of meditation: the loss of self in an inward journey to the center of our being, conducted in stillness and silence, with the common objective of all prayer—union with God. The unique or defining feature of contemplative prayer is the strong emphasis on letting go of all faculty functions of the intellect, mind, emotions, and imagination. There is no sense of reflecting on, focusing our attention on, or engaging our faculties on readings, images, or sacred objects. *It is a nonthinking approach, without words or images.* The focus is simply to create space to enable us to rest in God's presence and to ready ourselves to consent to God's action. The fundamental belief is that God is already present at the center of our being and that we need to empty ourselves to receive God's graces as they may be manifested to us. In this sense, as John teaches us, we "Make straight the way of the Lord,"[24] by clearing the path so we can more fully rest in God's presence and be ready to consent to God's action.

There is no question that contemplative prayer can pose quite a challenge. We are simply not used to shutting down our faculties, and meditating or praying without words. The assumption is that for many of us, contemplative prayer may be a new practice that requires ongoing learning. Moreover, when we diminish our faculties, we are letting go of control, which is something most of us find very difficult to do. However, the challenge may be well worth pursuing as many Christians have found the practice of contemplative prayer can become a helpful and transformative form of meditation in our spiritual journey to be one with God.

Centering Prayer

A question that arises on a frequent basis is: "What is the difference between contemplative prayer and centering prayer?" My best understanding is that centering prayer is an example of contemplative

---

24. John 1:23.

Toward an Understanding of Prayer

prayer. This means that in Figure 2, centering prayer would be a circle *within* the contemplative prayer domain.

Centering prayer is a widely adopted form of meditation in the West that was developed and taught by the late Fr. Thomas Keating and his colleagues, Fr. William Meninger and Fr. Basil Pennington. As in contemplative prayer, centering prayer involves letting go of all thoughts, reasoning, and reflection in stillness and silence, with the sole focus of resting in God's presence and consenting to God's action in stillness and silence.

A central issue seems to lie in understanding the use of what is referred to in centering prayer as the *sacred word*. The idea of the sacred word is not so much its meaning as its *intent* to be present, open, and responsive to God, who dwells within. That is, the sacred word is used to direct our attention to the presence of God within. Examples of sacred words include: God; Jesus; my Lord and my God; here I am Lord; come Lord Jesus; amen; etc. In centering prayer, the sacred word or phrase is used in getting started in the meditation by expressing the intention of being with God at the center of our being. It is also recommended that the chosen sacred word or phrase be used to gently bring our mind back to our intention when we realize we are distracted. It is important to understand that the sacred word or phrase is not meant to be an object of attention for our thinking mind. Nor is it meant to be a mantra, something to absorb our attention through unceasing repetition. Rather, it serves solely to express our *intention* to remain in the presence and action of God. Keating is particularly adamant on this point when he states:

> The meaning of the sacred word or its resonances should not be pursued. It is not chosen for its content but for its intent. It is better to choose a word that does not stir up other associations in your mind or cause you to consider its particular emotional qualities. The sacred word is only a gesture, an expression of your will's intention; it has no meaning other than your intention.[25]

---

25. Keating, *Open Mind, Open Heart*, 40.

In effect, I see centering prayer as a form of contemplative prayer distinct from the other approaches to meditation briefly described above (guided meditation, Ignatian meditation, prayer of the heart, discursive meditation, and transcendental meditation).

In sum, the defining features of contemplative prayer, as used in this book, can be described as an approach in meditation that is:

- nonthinking
- designed to empty oneself of thoughts and emotions
- conducted in stillness and silence
- focused on the presence of God within
- a readying of ourselves to consent to God's action, either during the prayer session or later during the course of the day
- intended to create space within oneself to become, with God's grace, one with God.

Reviewing One's Practice

It is clear there are several approaches available to Christians as they try to develop a lifelong practice of prayer. It is most important that you examine your own prayer practice to review what you have in place presently so as to see what may be added or enhanced.

In my own case, it wasn't so much what was not working as it was what was missing. I concluded that church-based practices—Mass, Eucharist, and other group services—were insufficient for me. I needed something more private and personal, not to replace the group practices, but to be added to them. As I looked at meditation, I found some of the approaches too busy and too structured. I felt I was missing the dimension of stillness—especially internal stillness. The approach of contemplative prayer seemed to meet these needs for me—especially internal stillness and silence (nonthinking and nonattention to words, thoughts, or objects); and a focus or resting in God's presence and consenting to God's action.

Toward an Understanding of Prayer

The remainder of this book is designed to explore more fully, and to deepen our understanding and practice of, contemplative prayer.

For Personal Application

1. What church-based or group prayer are you presently engaged with?
2. What meditation approaches have you used?
3. What are the challenges you face with maintaining your present prayer practices?
4. What prayer practices, group or individual, do you plan to examine and enhance?
5. What aspects of contemplative prayer have you practiced?
6. What aspects of contemplative prayer do you feel you need to add to your practice?

> **Action Response:** Is there something *specific* in this chapter that draws you to make a change in, or add to, your spiritual journey?

Section Two

Erecting the Pillars

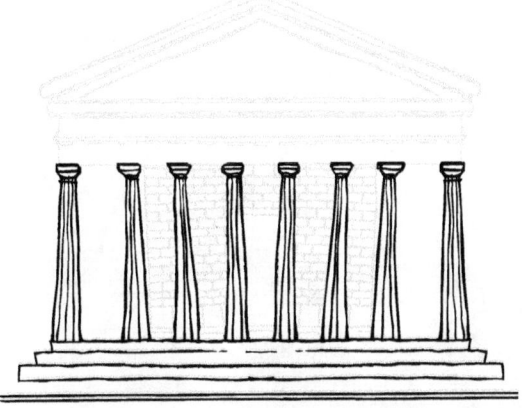

ONCE THE FOUNDATIONS OF contemplative prayer are in place, the next step is to erect the pillars. While there may well be other pillars to prayer in general, in this book three critical areas are identified as central to contemplative prayer—the divine indwelling, stillness and silence, and detachment. These factors come into play because of the very nature of contemplative prayer, as it involves a journey inwards to the center of our being where God resides, and recognizing the need to remove obstructions to this journey. The assumption is that if these pillars are systematically addressed and better understood we will be in a much stronger position to effectively adopt the implementation details described in Section 3 for developing and sustaining a contemplative prayer practice.

3

The Divine Indwelling

It is the Spirit who makes us one with God and in God . . . We have all received the same Spirit, enlivening us and causing us to be in Christ, in the Father, in the Spirit. We are in God and God is in us . . .[1]

—THOMAS KEATING

SUPPOSE WE WERE TO ask today's Christian this question: "Where would you find God?" I suspect a common response would be: "God is everywhere," or "God is omnipresent." Then suppose we added, "Can you give me an example?" Responses would likely be: "In the heavens," "In nature," "In the goodness of people," "In special events and celebrations, such as the birth of a child," and "In church services, sacraments, or prayers." I wonder at what point would someone say, "Within ourselves." My suspicion would be that the belief of the presence of God within, may not receive much attention—the majority or responses would center on God being outside of ourselves. My sense is that Christians, by and large, would call themselves "seekers" in that they wish to find God and center their lives on God—that there is a *longing* for God. Yet,

---

1. Keating, *Mystery of Christ*, 92.

Section Two: Erecting the Pillars

we don't fully acknowledge that God is already present *within us*. This situation reminds me of a talk given by Thomas Merton at the Sisters of Loretto Convent in 1962:

> And that is one of the great things to realize, that you don't have to go anywhere much in order to find Our Lord. We don't have to find Him because He comes to find us, you see; that is what we must remember most of all; we find Him by letting Him find us.[2]

Merton's simple message is that we don't have to "seek" God because God is already present within us. Or, as Meister Eckhart bluntly reminds us, "God is at home (in us), we are abroad."[3] In seeking God then, a needed focus is how to become more fully aware of, and responsive to, the presence of God within—*the divine indwelling*.

The focus in this chapter is to examine more closely the belief of the divine indwelling, or the presence of God within, and in particular the importance of this belief in relation to our prayer practice. Topics addressed include: 1) Divine indwelling in Scripture and spiritual writings, 2) oneness with God, 3) manifesting the glory of God, 4) suffering and the divine indwelling, 5) the myth of unworthiness, and 6) relevance to our prayer practice.

Divine Indwelling in Scripture and Spiritual Writings

Scripture

The Old Testament, in the Christian tradition frequently speaks to foretelling the coming of God in our midst through the incarnation of Jesus. There is the strong message that God is present, and ever watchful, with the promise of a richer and fuller presence:

> My presence will go with you and I will bring you rest.[4]

2. Thurston and Swain, *Hidden in the Same Mystery*, 10.
3. Eckhart, *Complete Mystical Works of Meister Eckhart*, 355.
4. Exod 33:14.

The Divine Indwelling

> God is in the midst of the city; it shall not be moved.... The Lord of hosts is with us; the God of Jacob is our refuge.[5]

> The Lord brought us out of Egypt with a mighty hand and an outstretched arm... and he brought us to this place and gave us this land, a land flowing with milk and honey.[6]

> And you shall build an altar there to the Lord your God of unhewn stones... rejoicing before the Lord your God.[7]

> And have them make me a sanctuary, so that I may dwell among them.[8]

The New Testament, through the incarnation, reveals that God is not only present among us, but resides *within us*—the gift of the *divine indwelling*:

> It is no longer I who live but it is Christ who lives in me.[9]

> May they all be one... may they be one in us, as you are in me and I in you... and they may be one as we are one.[10]

> ... you are in the Spirit because the Spirit of God dwells in you...[11]

> Abide in me as I abide in you. Just as the branch cannot bear fruit by itself unless it abides in the vine, neither can you unless you abide in me. I am the vine, you are the branches.[12]

> In him we live and move, and have our being.[13]

---

5. Ps 46:5, 11.
6. Deut 26:8–9.
7. Deut 27:5–7.
8. Exod 25:8.
9. Gal 2:20.
10. John 17:21–22.
11. Rom 8:9.
12. John 15:4–5.
13. Acts 17:28.

Section Two: Erecting the Pillars

Spiritual Writings

Paul Knitter summarizes the breadth and depth of spiritual writings on the subject of the divine indwelling over the centuries when he writes: "Christian mystical literature abounds with expressions such as 'one with Christ,' 'temples of the Holy Spirit,' 'the body of Christ,' 'spouses of Christ,' the 'Divine Indwelling,' and 'participants in the divine nature.'"[14]

Some of these spiriltual writings include:

Bishop Kallistos Ware:

If the hesychast strips his mind of all humanly devised concepts, so far as this is possible . . . that he may be filled with an all-embracing sense of the divine indwelling.[15]

Thomas Merton

The Christ we seek is within us, in our inmost self, is our inmost self, and yet infinitely transcends ourselves.[16]

Beatrice Bruteau

Let us also learn to turn the mind inward, to enter into our "inner chamber and shut the door" so as to seek the root of our being in secret. When the secret root has been found, it will show, for our life will be transformed. . . . We will not believe in ourselves as merely finite particular beings. We will know that we are rooted in the divine.[17]

---

14. Knitter, *Without Buddha I Could Not Be a Christian*, 17.
15. Ware, *Inner Kingdom*, 97.
16. Merton, "Letter to Daisetz T. Suzuki," 361.
17. Bruteau, *What Can We Learn from the East*, 28.

The Divine Indwelling

St. Teresa of Avila

> We need no wings to go in search of Him, but have only to look upon Him present within us.[18]

Oneness with God

When we seek God outside of ourselves, there is the implied assumption that God is a separate being—a relationship stipulated in terms of *dualism*. However, one of the most gratifying, and humbling, implications of the divine indwelling is that we are invited to become *one* with God—a limitless covenant of *nondualism*. St. Paul constantly reminds us of our call to conversion, to become one with Christ: "Let the same mind be in you that was in Christ Jesus."[19] In a similar way, clinical psychologist and retreat leader James Finley explains:

> We become the same as Christ Jesus in our minds through a lifelong process of conversion in which Christ's mind and our mind become one mind, one way of seeing and being in the world.[20]

Christians undertaking a spiritual path typically have a common goal of union with God. Thomas Merton describes this purpose as a journey of, "Apprehending him in a deep and vital experience which is beyond the reach of any natural understanding, is the reason for our creation by God."[21] If we take time to seriously consider that God already dwells within us, it should be apparent that union with God should be readily attainable. However, it is not that simple. The reason is that we are too busy attending to goals, objectives, and events outside of ourselves. The challenge is to effectively stop and give ourselves a chance to enter this space

---

18. St. Teresa of Avila, "Chapter 28," para.2.
19. Phil 2:5.
20. Finley, *Christian Meditation*, 175.
21. Merton, *Seeds of Contemplation*, 139.

Section Two: Erecting the Pillars

within ourselves where God resides and become one with God—to develop a *practice of contemplative prayer* where we rest in the presence and action of God within. We are given a profound opportunity to accept this astonishing gift of the divine indwelling and to *allow* ourselves to become one with God.

Manifesting the Glory of God

When we are mindful, the presence of God in our lives can be recogized in a number of ways such as: in the sheer beauty found in nature; the overwhelming kindnesses exhibited by so many people; the countless blessings that come into our lives; and in our spiritual practices. It is also important to consider how God's presence can be manifested *through us* because of the divine indwelling. By becoming one with God, we allow ourselves to be a temple, or a lighthouse, where God's glory shines through us to the world. Teilhard de Chardin, mystic and scientist, describes this gift in a powefully poetic way as he connects the divine indwelling with the world:

> Throughout my life, by means of my life, the world has little by little, caught fire in my sight until, aflame all around me, it has become almost completely luminous from within. . . . Such has been my experience in contact with the earth—the diaphany of the divine at the heart of the universe on fire . . . Christ; His heart; a fire: capable of penetrating everywhere and, gradually, spreading everywhere.[22]

Suffering and the Divine Indwelling

One of the the most difficult challenges facing Christians is reconciling the belief that God is present within us and around us with the suffering that is so pervasive in the world. For example, we can sit in the presence of a beautiful sunset or gaze at the profound beauty and vastness of the Grand Canyon, and yet we see

---

22. Chardin, *Divine Milieu*, editor's note, 9.

The Divine Indwelling

the shocking loss of life, lifelong injuries and suffering, and catastrophic devastation through natural disasters. We are presently experiencing global tragedies, hardships, and suffering through COVID-19, the devasting coronavirus that has infected millions of people and caused hundreds of thousands of deaths around the world, with no end in sight as yet. Then, perhaps hardest of all is to understand the divine indwelling when it comes to individuals who perpetrate heinous crimes against humanity. "Where is God?" we may ask in these situations, especially for those who suffer so greatly.

Perhaps some light can be shed on this mystery by examining the spiritual writings of those who have experienced sustained and profound levels of suffering. These authors inform us that we need to draw on God to help us to help ourselves through his sacred presence within us. That even under extreme conditions, God is present right there among the afflicted. Three exemplars of such authors come to mind immediately—Etty Hillesum, Elie Wiesel, and Dietrich Bonhoeffer, all of whom were victims of the monstrous concentration camps of Nazi Germany in World War II.

Etty Hillesum (1914–1943)—the Dutch author of letters and diaries, inspiring confidant, and the provider of compassionate support for so many prisoners—was executed in the Auschwitz concentration camp in 1943. In one of her letters she writes with poignant trust regarding the divine indwelling and suffering:

> But one thing is becoming increasingly clear to me: that You cannot help us, that we must help You to help ourselves. And that is all we can manage these days and also all that really matters: that we safeguard that little piece of You, God in ourselves . . . but we must help You and defend Your dwelling place within us to the last . . . but believe me I shall always labor for You and remain faithful to You and I shall never drive You from my presence.[23]

Holocaust survivor, prolific author, advocate, and 1986 Nobel Peace Prize winner Elie Wiesel (1928–2016) recounted this story from the Buchenwald prison camp when the prisoners

23. Hillesum, *Interrupted Life*, 178.

Section Two: Erecting the Pillars

were forced to march past the hanging of three victims—two men and a child:

> The three condemned prisoners together stepped onto the chairs. "Where is merciful God, where is He?" someone behind me was asking. The chairs were tipped over. Then came the march past. The two men were no longer alive... But the third rope was still moving: the child too light, was still breathing... And we were forced to look at him at close range...
>
> Behind me, I heard the same man asking: "For God's sake, where is God?" And from within me, I heard a voice answer: "Where He is? This is where—hanging here from these gallows."[24]

German pastor, theologian, and author Dietrich Bonhoeffer (1906–1945) was imprisoned and executed in the Flossenburg concentration camp for his alleged anti-Nazi activities. In his prison letters he teaches us that God's presence helps us to deal with suffering and also how to draw closer to God through suffering in this beautiful and powerful prayer: "May God in his mercy lead us through these times; but above all may he lead us to himself."[25]

Compassion is the flip side of suffering. That is, the victims are the ones who suffer directly while others may be moved to compassion. The challenge is: How does one have the strength and resources to display compassion under inhumane conditions where we have no control? Once again, we can turn to guidance from someone who has experienced and observed suffering. Simone Weil writes:

> In true love it is not we who love the afflicted in God: it is God in us who loves them. When we are in affliction, it is God in us who loves those who wish us well. Compassion and gratitude come down from God, and when they are exchanged in a glance, God is present at the point where the eyes of those who give and those who receive

---

24. Wiesel, *Night*, 64–65.
25. Bonhoeffer, *Letters and Papers from Prison*, 19.

The Divine Indwelling

meet . . . That is why it comes about only through the agency of God.[26]

One thing we can be sure of: suffering abounds and it is part and parcel of *everyone's* life—though for some more than others. We also struggle with trying to make sense of suffering and the prevalence of evil in the world. While we should try to do what we can to alleviate the suffering, which may or may not bear results, we must also see it as a *grace*, something to draw us closer to God and to trust in God's steadfast love. The mystery of suffering is an integral part of our spiritual pathway.

Myth of Unworthiness

A common way we limit the efficacy of the divine indwelling is to assume that we are unworthy of the divine presence within. We don't quite accept that we are temples of God. One reason is that we become too aware of our own failings. Perhaps we committed some serious wrong, or we are just too mindful of our nagging shortcomings—character defects that keep surfacing. Unfortunately, when we think this way, we are operating on the assumption that we, by ourselves, can change our behavior, or that we cannot change and have to live with these problems, have to be cognizant of their limitations.

Rather, we need to accept that God's steadfast love is for everyone, without exception. Scripture is rich in reminding us frequently that God's love is always there for us and that God's gifts help us to transcend our own failings:

> Give thanks to the Lord, for he is good, for his steadfast love endures forever.[27]

> But God, who is rich in mercy, out of the great love with which he loved us even when we were dead through our trespasses, made us alive together with Christ—by grace

---

26. Weil, *Waiting for God*, 93–94.
27. Ps 118:1.

> you have been saved—and raised us up with him and seated us with him in the heavenly places in Christ Jesus.[28]

> May the Lord direct your hearts to the love of God and to the steadfastness of Christ.[29]

The spiritual pathway requires us to forego our own inclinations and delusions. We have to accept that we cannot take care of our problems by ourselves and trust that in following the spiritual path our problems can be attenuated. That is, we become open and responsive to God's steadfast love and mercy. Thomas Merton, in examining the parable of the prodigal son, writes:

> Mercy is also fidelity; it is also strength. It is the faithful and indefectible mercy of God . . . It is the power that binds us to God because He has promised us mercy and will never fail us in His Promise.[30]

Once again, we are faced with the belief that God's love and mercy are *gifts*—gratuitous graces that are not earned by our efforts. Merton summarizes this issue of our worthiness of God's love and forgiveness in a telling way when he writes:

> Revelation of the mercy of God makes the whole problem of worthiness something almost laughable.[31]

Relevance to Our Prayer Practice

The belief in the divine indwelling, once more fully realized, will have a significant impact on the way we pray. This is not to say we need to abandon the way we have been praying. Rather, it is that we may be given the grace of an additional way to pray, which I am calling *contemplative prayer*. Jesus gave us the lead when he instructed his disciples: "But whenever you pray, go into your room

---

28. Eph 2:4–6.
29. 2 Thess 3:5.
30. Merton, *Seasons of Celebration*, 175.
31. Merton, *New Seeds of Contemplation*, 75.

The Divine Indwelling

and shut the door and pray to your Father who is in secret; and your Father who sees in secret will reward you."[32] The symbolism is powerful. Going to "your room" represents an inward journey to our center where God resides. "Shutting the door" means leaving outside our thoughts, words, images, plans, and everything to do with the outside world. Once inside, with the door shut, we put ourselves in the presence of God and wait on the "Father who sees us" and who will bless us. Our role becomes one of sitting, waiting, looking, and simply resting in the presence of God, without words, and consenting to God's action as it may be presented to us then and throughout the day.

For Personal Application

1. What is your answer to the question, "Where do you find God?"
2. What does the divine indwelling mean to you?
3. What is your sense of your oneness with God?
4. How do you deal with suffering in your life and with suffering in the lives of others?
5. To what extent can you accept that God's steadfast love is always available regardless of your own failings?

> **Action Response:** Is there something *specific* in this chapter that draws you to make a change in, or add to, your spiritual journey?

---

32. Matt 6:6.

4

Necessity of Stillness and Silence

Somewhere in those depths of silence I came upon my first experiences of God as a loving presence that was always near, and prayer as simple trust in that presence.[1]

—CYNTHIA BOURGEAULT

ON ONE LEVEL, CONTEMPLATIVE prayer should be reasonably straightforward because God is so willing and available to bestow the gift of prayer upon us and he is already dwelling within us. Unfortunately, our experience tells us this is not necessarily the case. A major reason is that to be ready to receive this gift from God we need to make an *inward journey* that requires a level of withdrawing from all the *external factors* involved with daily living that can fully occupy our time, such as: our career, family, relationships, recreational needs, unresolved conflicts, paying our bills, etc. In addition, we also have to let go of *internal factors* that can readily consume our minds, such as thoughts that almost automatically center on past or future events. Practitioners often report that no sooner are they situated for meditation than their "monkey

---

1. Bourgeault, *Centering Prayer*, 5.

mind" takes over, that is, their thoughts become incessant and all over the place. Others report that emotions quickly come to the surface once they stop and try to meditate. Feelings of resentment, worry, anxiety, and anger toward something readily surface that seem to be more intense and present than at other times during their day. It is clear these external and internal factors can pose a daunting challenge to Christians seeking to establish a contemplative prayer practice.

The purpose of this chapter is to explore what we can do to facilitate this inward journey given these challenges. From what we have learned in reading Scripture and spiritual writings, along with conversations with some practitioners, one point is clear: we need to establish, as best we can, *silence* and *stillness* in our practice. This focus is a prerequisite condition for increasing our capacity in making this inward journey and in readying ourselves to become one with God. Topics examined are: 1) The need for stillness and silence in Scripture and spiritual writings, and 2) dissonance between stillness and silence with prevailing cultural norms.

Need for Stillness and Silence in Scripture and Spiritual Writings

Both Scripture and writings from spiritual leaders emphasize the necessity of stillness and silence in our prayer life. It is helpful to reflect on these writings to heighten our awareness of the need to do what we can to establish stillness and silence in our prayer practice and in our lives in general.

Scripture

Old Testament

Be still before the Lord, and wait patiently for him.[2]

2. Ps 37:7.

Section Two: Erecting the Pillars

The Lord will fight for you, and you have only to keep still.[3]

Be still and know that I am God.[4]

Be silent, all people, before the Lord; for he has roused himself from his holy dwelling.[5]

New Testament

But whenever you pray, go into your room and shut the door and pray to your Father who is in secret; and your Father who sees in secret will reward you.[6]

Rather let your adornment be the inner self with the lasting beauty of a gentle and quiet spirit, which is very precious in God's eyes.[7]

In the morning, while it was still very dark, he got up and went out to a deserted place, and there he prayed.[8]

But he [Jesus] would withdraw to deserted places and pray.[9]

Jesus went out to a mountainside to pray, and spent the night praying to God. When morning came, he called his disciples to him and chose twelve of them.[10]

---

3. Exod 14:14.
4. Ps 46:10.
5. Zech 2:13.
6. Matt 6:6.
7. 1 Pet 3:4.
8. Mark 1:35.
9. Luke 5:16.
10. Luke 6:12–13.

Necessity of Stillness and Silence

Spiritual Writings

William Johnston

There is a still point of the spirit to which no man, no devil, no angel can penetrate: it is the preserve of God alone.[11]

Thomas Keating

The root of prayer is interior silence.[12]

Michael Casey

Prayer is not a matter of actively thinking about God ... What is important here is simply to appreciate that prayer demands a certain stillness of mind and silence of thoughts.[13]

Brian Taylor

Contemplative prayer, then, is a gift from God, for which we prepare ourselves by sitting in silence and inviting the work of the spirit within us.[14]

Carolyn Myss

Quiet does not satisfy the soul—only silence does.[15]

11. Johnston, *Mysticism of the Cloud of Unknowing*, 174.
12. Keating, *Open Mind, Open Heart*, 12.
13. Casey, *Toward God*, 38.
14. Taylor, *Becoming Christ*, 7.
15. Myss, *Entering the Castle*, 88.

Section Two: Erecting the Pillars

Martin Laird

> A sailor practices sailing skills that harness the gift of wind that brings the sailor home,
> but there is nothing the sailor can do to make the wind blow. And so, it is with contemplative
> prayer, not a technique, but a skill. The skill required is interior silence.[16]

Phileena Heuertz

> The heart of Christian contemplation beats with silence and expands our consciousness.[17]

Dissonance between Stillness and Silence with Prevailing Cultural Norms

The place of silence and stillness in society today reminds me of an experience I had a few years back when I was attending a conference in a major city. When I retired for the evening, I was overwhelmed by the traffic noise, what with the roar of engines, blaring horns, and constant sirens from emergency and police vehicles. This incessant noise was only broken by the thermostatically controlled heating unit in the room that would engage, periodically, with a burst of mechanical rattling noise throughout the entire night. Needless to say, I got little to no sleep. To cap off my stay, I stopped at a nearby coffee shop for a pastry and coffee and to start the day by reading the local paper. I was greeted with music in the coffee shop that was so loud I had to shout my order to the server. Unable to cope with the noise from the music and loud conversations, I took my order, left the coffee shop, and read the paper at a later time. This experience of relentless noise made me acutely

---

16. Laird, *Into the Silent Land*, 4.
17. Heuertz, *Mindful Silence*, 8.

Necessity of Stillness and Silence

aware of the pervasiveness of noise in our society. I began to reflect on how many commuters used headphones and the high numbers of students with their smart phones and mobile devices and ear plugs for the occasions when they have to wait a few minutes, or when they need to ride or walk somewhere. George Prochnik, researcher on the effect of noise on health, reports the alarming deleterious effects of increasing noise in society on our physical health—hearing loss, in particular—and on our psychological, social, and spiritual needs. He examines the effect of a noise-filled society on the loss of silence, describes the importance of silence to our deliberations, thinking, reading, and general well-being, and raises this critical question:

> Why, I wondered, does there appear a growing consensus about the benefits of silence and yet at the same time as the world seems, on so many fronts, to be getting noisier?[18]

One of the biggest traps we can fall into is to become inured to, or accepting of, our world becoming noisier. That is, we end up just paying token recognition to the importance of silence in our lives and especially in our prayer life. A rector has not forgotten the following instance that brought this issue home to him in a telling manner:

> A guest pastor from India commented after a Sunday service at Grace: "Dear brother, your beautiful Sunday worship service began with singing 'Let all mortal flesh keep silence,' followed by 60 minutes of uninterrupted speech." He caught the irony of what we missed, our singing about awe-filled silence before God and our structured avoidance of doing so.[19]

Similarly, a parish priest shared with me his concern regarding the absence of silence at Sunday Masses. He then decided to include a period of three minutes of silence following the reading of the gospel, the sermon, and reception of communion. He also shortened his sermon to avoid lengthening the service overall.

18. Prochnik, *In Pursuit of Silence*, 14–15.
19. Alban Institute, "Silence," para. 1.

Section Two: Erecting the Pillars

He became acutely aware of the unrest in the church during these short periods of silence. He also mentioned several parishioners complained that these periods of silence were not helpful and interrupted the flow of the Mass. So, the practice was dropped.

Just as with silence, there is a similar clash between our cultural norms and the practice of *stillness*. Once again, we live in a society with an ever-increasing busyness that is not only the norm, but which has become highly valued. If we are busy, then things are going well—we are being productive and useful. If things are slow, then we have problems. When we ask someone, "How was your day?" the preferred response is, "Busy, busy, busy." A common remark from retired folk is, "I can't believe how busy I am," or "I am so busy I don't know how I ever got anything done when I was working." By the same rule, if we are not busy, we often become restless and feel unfulfilled or guilty. So, we scramble to try to find things to occupy ourselves.

It is interesting to see that the consuming busyness and its impact on the spiritual life has been a perennial problem. For example, the following excerpt is attributed to Julian of Norwich, a fourteenth-century mystic and spiritual writer, who wrote this prayer that still speaks to us today:

> Lord, let not our souls be busy inns that have no room for thee or thine,
> But quiet homes of prayer and praise, where thou mayest find fit company,
> Where the needful cares of life are wisely ordered and put away,
> And wide, sweet spaces kept for thee; where holy thoughts pass up and down
> And fervent longings watch and wait thy coming.[20]

It is quite evident that our society, with its trend of becoming noisier, busier, and more rushed, can pose serious difficulties to our ability to cultivate the practice of stillness and silence, especially in our prayer life. Yet we must remain cognizant of the strong reminders in Scripture and in spiritual writings that we need to create stillness and silence to set the stage for prayer in

---

20. Julian of Norwich, as quoted in Alban Institute, "Silence," para. 9.

Necessity of Stillness and Silence

general, and contemplative prayer in particular. This means we need to take direct, planned, and effective steps in order to establish a prayer practice that involves stillness and silence. In other words, we cannot expect to find moments of silence and stillness in our day. Rather, we must create such moments. Specific details regarding strategies for establishing stillness and silence during designated times for contemplative prayer and throughout the day are described in the three chapters of Section 3, Building the Temple—your contemplative prayer practice. In this way we may approach the ideal taught by Thomas Merton that, "Every moment and every event of every man's life on earth plants something in his soul."[21]

For Personal Application

1. How does your typical day look in relation to silence, stillness, and busyness?
2. Do any of the Scripture or spiritual writers' citations have strong meaning for you?
3. Have the concerns of stillness, silence, and busyness affected your prayer life? If so, in what way(s)?
4. What steps have you taken to address the need for stillness and silence in your day and in your prayer life?

> **Action Response**: Is there something *specific* in this chapter that draws you to make a change in, or add to, your spiritual journey?

---

21. Merton, *New Seeds of Contemplation*, 14.

5

Spiritual Pathway

Paved with Detachment

Our desires and aversions are mercurial rulers. They demand to be pleased. Desire commands us to run off and get what we want. Aversion insists that we must avoid the things that repel us . . . Desire and aversion, though powerful, are just habits. And we can train ourselves to have better habits . . . Do your best to rein in your habits.[1]

—EPICTETUS

A MAJOR OBSTACLE IN undertaking our inward journey to communion with God is attachments—the desire for material possessions, recognition, honor, accomplishments, power, success, wealth, comfort, and the satisfaction of physical wants or needs. In addition, we can spend considerable energy in avoiding situations in our day that we find aversive, such as: paying bills; doing certain chores, exercising and taking care of our health, reporting problems at work, and spending more time with certain people. Letting go of these attachments and facing these difficult situations become both a critical

---

1. Epictetus, *Manual for Living*, 12–13.

Spiritual Pathway

first step and an ongoing challenge, not only as we engage in meditation, but as we commit to a lifelong spiritual journey.

Not so long ago, a good friend said to me, "What, in one sentence, do you think is the most important step we can take in meditation?" I replied, "Get out of the way." I went on to explain that one of the major attachments I had to deal with, and still struggle with, is the need to be in control, to set the expectations and make prayer happen the way I want it to. In my career as a research associate and professional development provider for educators I took pride in setting goals and objectives, mapping out procedural details to accomplish these goals and objectives, and establishing measures to determine if these expectations had been met. In other words, to a large extent, I felt in control of the development and execution of the plans and the desired outcomes.

Naturally, I approached my meditation practice in much the same way. I studied and tried different forms of meditation, settling on contemplative prayer. I knew what I wanted—deeper union with God, with more order and calm in my life. I felt I knew what to do from studying and practicing various methods. So, did I accomplish my goals? Of course not! I soon felt I was getting nowhere. During a personal conference at a retreat, the leader told me I was: "Intellectualizing too much" and that I needed to "let go of [my] attachment to being in control and allow the Spirit to work." I began to learn that I needed to get out of the way.

The message I was trying to communicate to my friend was that we have so many attachments that, sadly, define us and constitute a major obstacle to our receptivity to the grace of union with God. These attachments need to be addressed if we wish to fully embrace the Christian pathway.

The purpose of this chapter is to develop a deeper understanding of the roles attachments play in our spiritual journey and what is involved in dealing with them. In a word—*detachment*. Topics that will be addressed are: 1) Exhortations in Scripture and spiritual writings, 2) the true self and the false self, and 3) the practice of letting go.

Section Two: Erecting the Pillars

Exhortations in Scripture and Spiritual Writings

Both Scripture and spiritual writings are replete with teachings on the need to practice detachment from all aspects of ourselves that get in the way of our openness and receptivity to the call of union with God.

Scripture

Trust in the Lord with all your heart, and do not rely on your own insight. In all your ways acknowledge him, and he will make straight your paths.[2]

If any want to become my followers, let them deny themselves and take up their cross and follow me.[3]

A certain ruler asked him, "Good Teacher, what must I do to inherit eternal life?" Jesus said to him, "Why do you call me good? No one is good but God alone. You know the commandments: 'You shall not commit adultery; You shall not murder; You shall not steal; You shall not bear false witness; Honor your father and mother.'" He replied, "I have kept all these since my youth." When Jesus heard this, he said to him, "There is still one thing lacking. Sell all that you own and distribute the money to the poor, and you will have treasure in heaven; then come, follow me."[4]

Blessed are the poor in spirit, for theirs is the kingdom of heaven.[5]

Do not worry about anything, but in everything, by prayer and supplication, with thanksgiving, let your requests be made known to God. And the peace of God,

---

2. Prov 3:5–6.
3. Matt 16:24.
4. Luke 18:18–22.
5. Matt 5:3.

Spiritual Pathway

which surpasses all understanding, will guard your hearts and your minds in Christ Jesus.[6]

Spiritual Writings

Thomas Merton

Only when we are able to "let go" of everything within us, all desire to see, to know, to taste and to experience the presence of God, do we truly become able to experience that presence with the overwhelming conviction and reality that revolutionize our entire inner life.[7]

Dorothy Day

If you believe in the mission of Jesus Christ, then you're bound to try to let go of your past, in the sense you are entitled to his forgiveness. To keep regretting what was is to deny God's grace.[8]

Meister Eckhart

Now you may ask what this detachment is that is so noble in itself. You should know that true detachment is nothing else but a mind that stands unmoved by all accidents of joy or sorrow, honor, shame, or disgrace, as a mountain of lead stands unmoved by a breath of wind. This immovable detachment brings a man into the greatest likeness of God.[9]

---

6. Phil 4:6–7.
7. Merton, *Climate of Monastic Prayer*, 111.
8. Day, *Reckless Way of Love*, 63.
9. Eckhart, *Complete Mystical Works of Meister Eckhart*, 568–69.

Section Two: Erecting the Pillars

Evelyn Underhill

To live the spiritual life, it means subordinating all other interests to that single fact.[10]

Etty Hillesum

And now that I don't want to own anything anymore and am free, now I suddenly own everything, now my inner riches are immeasurable.[11]

Tom Stella

We can more freely let go of what we have when we are aware of the inner richness we possess.[12]

The True Self and the False Self

The *true self/false self* has been a helpful construct used in Eastern spiritual writings for centuries, and more recently in Western Christianity. The true self is identified as the self that was made in the "image and likeness of God,"[13] and thereby realized fully when it becomes one with God. Thomas Merton, recognized as a leading proponent of the true self/false self paradigm in Christian literature, describes the true self as:

> . . . the pure glory of God in us. . . . It is like a pure diamond, blazing with the invisible light of heaven. It is in everybody, and if we could see these billions of points of light coming together in the face and blaze of a sun, that

10. Underhill, *Spiritual Life*, 85.
11. Hillesum, *Interrupted Life*, 16.
12. Stella, *God Instinct*, 97.
13. Gen 1:27.

Spiritual Pathway

would make all the darkness and cruelty of life vanish completely.[14]

By contrast, the *false self* refers to the self that is identified with and limited to what is external, such as events, possessions, careers, pleasures, and accomplishments. Merton describes the false self in this way:

> Every one of us is shadowed by an illusory person: a false self. . . . My false and private self is the one who wants to exist outside the reach of God's will and God's love—outside of reality and outside of life. And such a life cannot help but be an illusion. We are not very good at recognizing illusions, least of all the ones we cherish about ourselves.[15]

In general, a useful way to discriminate between the true self and the false self at a personal level is to ask this question: "What is your center?" In the case of the true self, God is the center, whereas for the false self, one's ego is the center. Most of us would likely say our center is somewhere between the true and the false selves. That is, while we feel committed to making God our center, our true self, we are aware of impeding attachments that put the focus on our ego—our false self. The challenge becomes, "What can we do to minimize the control the false self has over our daily lives?" Or, "What can we do to transform the false self so that it does not provide obstacles on our spiritual pathway?" The answer lies in the need to develop the virtue of *detachment*. Jesus' guidelines are very clear on this need in his teachings. For example:

> If any want to become my followers, let them deny themselves [*false self*], and take up their cross and follow me [*true self*].[16]

---

14. Merton, *Conjectures of a Guilty Bystander*, 158.
15. Merton, *New Seeds of Contemplation*, 34.
16. Matt 16:14.

Section Two: Erecting the Pillars

The Practice of Letting Go

Conceptually the practice of letting go of attachments related to the false self makes perfect sense. How can we ready ourselves to receive the gift of union with God if we are attending to, or consumed by, needs of the false self, such as greed, ambition, recognition, status, having our own way, anger, resentments, jealousy, and so on? Clearly, while we are focused, at whatever level, on aspects of the false self, we limit not only our ability to *listen* to the call of God, but also our capacity to *consent*. The practice of letting go has important relevance to many areas of the spiritual path. Richard Rohr, Franciscan priest and founder of the Center of Action and Contemplation, writes: "All great spirituality is about letting go."[17] The practice of detachment has several ramifications for our spiritual journey, and in particular our contemplative prayer practice, and are briefly described as: a) Perspective: the reality of transience, b) letting go and letting be, c) consenting to God's action: letting go of our own will, d) living in the present moment: letting go the past and future, e) living with uncertainty, and f) the neeed for forgiveness.

Perspective—The Reality of Transience

It is illogical, when we pause to consider it, that we can become so driven to attain attachments and cling to so much in our lives when we only have them for a finite time. Moreover, we live in such a transient society that what is sought after today is obsolete tomorrow. The Greek philosopher Heraclitus, as far back as 500 BCE, taught that nothing is stable and all is in flux: "By cosmic rule ... all things change, ... The river where you set your foot just now is gone—those waters giving way to this, now this."[18] Attention to this transience of life is central to all major religions. For example, in Buddhism, the Buddha speaks of *impermanence*; in Judaism, the Torah describes life in terms of *sojournings*; in Islam, references are

---

17. Rohr, *Spring within Us*, 228.
18. Heraclitus, *Fragments*, xii.

noted in the Qu'ran that everything *perishes*; and in Christianity, Scripture reminds us that we do not have a *lasting city.*

In many respects, our lives can be seen as fleeting moments. This means we need to maximize the opportunities we have for growing in union with God and developing practices to address the multiple attachments that impede this journey. Jack Kornfield, one of the key teachers to introduce Buddhist mindfulness practice to the West, captures this perspective of transience and detachment with this meaningful story:

> There is an old story about a famous rabbi living in Europe who was visited one day by a man who had traveled by ship from New York to see him. The man came to the great rabbi's dwelling, a large house on a street in a European city, and was directed to the rabbi's room, which was in the attic. He entered to find the master living in a room with a bed, a chair, and a few books. The man had expected much more. After greetings, he asked, "Rabbi, where are your things?" The rabbi asked in return, "Well, where are yours?" His visitor replied, "But, Rabbi, I'm only passing through," and the master answered, "So am I, so am I."[19]

Letting Go and Letting Be

Jon Kabat-Zinn, founder of Center for Mindfulness in Medicine, provides us with a helpful description of what it means to let go:

> Letting go means letting be. It does not mean pushing things away or forcing ourselves to release what we are clinging to, what we are most strongly attached to. On the contrary, letting go is akin to nonattachment, and in particular, nonattachment to outcome, when we are no longer grasping for what we want that we are already clinging to or what we simply *have* to have ... When you

---

19. Kornfield, "Letting Go," para. 6 (emphasis original).

Section Two: Erecting the Pillars

let things be as they are, you are aligning yourself with that domain of awareness itself, pure awareness.[20]

Consenting to God's Action—
Letting Go of Our Own Will

Contemplative prayer is described throughout this book as resting in the *presence* and *action* of God. The belief in the divine indwelling gives clear meaning to resting in the presence of God. However, what does it mean to rest in the presence of God's *action*? The answer lies in letting go of the attachments of the false self, and engaging with our whole heart in consenting to the will of God—becoming our *true self*.

The step of consenting to God's action, or God's will for us, can pose quite a challenge to many seekers as there is something daunting about abandoning our will. Moreover, we often experience the tension from not knowing what God's will is in many life situations. In fact, this confusion is a necessary part of the process of letting go of our own will and trusting in the will of God. Jean-Pierre de Caussade, French Catholic spiritual director and author of spiritual classics, explains the necessity of letting go of our own will in order to attain pure love of God when he writes:

> No thought, no mental effort, will teach us anything about pure love. We can learn of it only through the activity of God, and God teaches us, both through our reason and through our difficulties and setbacks . . . To know this, we must get rid of all we hold dear. We must strip ourselves of everything . . . We must reach the stage when all that the world contains ceases to exist and God is everything to us.[21]

---

20. Kabat-Zinn, *Mindfulness for Beginners*, 132–33.
21. Caussade, *Abandonment to Divine Providence*, 74.

Spiritual Pathway

Living in the Present Moment—
Letting Go of the Past and Future

It has been said that the vast majority of our thoughts center on certain aspects of our past or on future events. Ironically, we live in the present, yet our thoughts are anchored in the past or future. A useful analogue is the way our vision works—that is the connection between our focus and peripheral vision. When we look at something, say a picture on the wall, we clearly see the picture—the *focus*. At the same time, we see several objects around the picture, such as other objects farther away on the wall, on the floor, and in the general area—*peripheral vision*. However, while we are aware of objects in our peripheral vision, our attention and concentration are on the particular focus. It is not hard to imagine the confusion and problems there would be if we reversed this arrangement. That is, if we only attend to, or concentrate on, what we see in the periphery and have just a general awareness of what we are looking at. People would say of us in these situations that we have a blank look, or seem distant and preoccupied. The same is true when we dwell on the past or future when we are engaged with something in the present moment. We distort the relationship between the present moment and that of the past or future. The challenge is to *focus* on the present moment and to be aware of, but not concentrate on, the past or future. That is, the present needs to be the *focus*, and the past and future become the *peripheral vision*.

This does not mean one needs to be reciting prayers or reflecting on sacred thoughts while peeling the potatoes. But it does mean that peeling the potatoes is to be seen as sacred activity—the focal point of our concentration. That is, the presence of God becomes manifest in these so-called ordinary events of life. This perspective of a focus on the ordinary activities of the day was captured in a colorful yet striking way by Thomas Merton when he described his typical day in the monastery as, "What I wear is pants. What I do is live. How I pray is breathe."[22] Similarly, Thomas

---

22. Merton, *Day of a Stranger*, 41.

Section Two: Erecting the Pillars

Keating summarizes the transformation of ordinary activities into graced opportunities when he writes:

> As your sensitivity to the spiritual dimension of your being develops . . . you may begin to find the awareness of God's presence arising at times in ordinary activity. You may feel called to turn interiorly to God without knowing why . . . Without deliberately thinking of God, you may find that God is often present in the midst of your daily occupations.[23]

Living with Uncertainty

One of the certainties we all face in our spiritual journey is the experience that is best described as *uncertain*. We have an innate need to find answers, solve problems, and obtain closure. At one level, we need to deal effectively with uncertainties for survival, such as issues that affect safety, security, health, and financial and general well-being. However, there are many situations where solutions or directions are unclear and we are stuck with having to live with *unknowns*. While we may yearn for solutions in these cases, these unknowns can become graced opportunities given we are prepared to *let go* of our need for solutions through our own efforts alone, and embrace the problems as an integral part of our spiritual journey. I coauthored a recent book with my friend and colleague Pat Foley on issues of dealing with personal paradoxes, and concluded that:

> Living with the experience of paradoxes is a grace—a gift from God. Paradoxes, with all their encumbrances, can become a gateway to experience more fully the presence and action of God in our lives. Granted, it is a challenge to accept that confusion and suffering are opportunities to grow and become more transformed in our spiritual path to union with God. When we let go of the paradoxes, and turn them over to God, we may experience in

---

23. Keating, *Open Mind, Open Heart*, 23.

a more profound way a transformation which helps us to follow the Christian way of life more faithfully.[24]

Need for Forgiveness

We are all familiar with the quote from the celebrated poet Alexander Pope, "To err is human; to forgive is divine."[25] The common interpretation of this line is that all of us can and will make mistakes and that we need to forgive those who make the mistakes, just as God shows divine mercy in forgiving our misdeeds whatever they may be. Unfortunately, we are also very much aware of how difficult it is to forgive others, especially for the more serious offenses and for misdeeds directed to us personally. In these cases, it is not uncommon to harbor resentment, anger, or thoughts of retaliation and revenge. Yet, we are very familiar with Jesus's teaching in the Lord's prayer and in other sermons to, "forgive us our trespasses as we forgive those who trespass against us . . ."[26] The challenge lies in the *letting go of negative feelings* we have towards the individual(s) who has/have "erred" and turn the concerns over to the mercy and forgiveness of God, as St. Paul teaches, "and be kind to one another, tenderhearted, forgiving one another, as God in Christ has forgiven you."[27]

It is clear that forgiving others can pose a formidable challenge; however, forgiving *oneself* can be even more daunting. Again, we are faced with the need to *let go* of the feelings of guilt, inadequacy, depression, or despair, and trust in the healing power of God's mercy and steadfast love so clearly expressed in the teachings of St. Paul and the Psalms:

> But he said to me, "My grace is sufficient for you, for power is made perfect in weakness." So, I will boast all the more gladly of my weaknesses, so that the power of

24. Colvin and Foley, *Living with Paradoxes*, 97.
25. Pope, *Essay on Criticism*, Part II, para. 18.
26. Matt 6:12.
27. Eph 4:32.

Section Two: Erecting the Pillars

Christ may dwell in me. Therefore, I am content with weaknesses, insults, hardships, persecutions, and calamities for the sake of Christ; for whenever I am weak, then I am strong.[28]

The Lord is near to the brokenhearted and saves the crushed in spirit.[29]

Detachment is an essential practice in the spiritual pathway and has particular relevance to the development of contemplative prayer. The challenge is twofold. First, we must have the capacity to *let go* of anything that becomes an obstacle in our journey to union with God, and second, as we let go, we must put our trust in God's presence and action.

For Personal Application

1. What attachments do you consider to be strongest in your life?
2. How do you see attachments hindering your spiritual journey?
3. Do any of the Scripture or spiritual writers' citations have strong meaning for you?
4. What steps have you taken to let go of any particular attachments?
5. What situations do you find most challenging to forgive?

Action Response: Is there something *specific* in this chapter that draws you to make a change in, or add to, your spiritual journey?

---

28. 2 Cor 12:9–10.
29. Ps 34:18.

Section Three

Building the Temple

THE PREVIOUS TWO SECTIONS, laying the foundations and erecting the pillars, addressed recommended structures that should be in place for establishing a contemplative prayer practice. Now it is time to add the specific steps for building the temple—*your contemplative prayer practice*. The procedural details presented in the following three chapters describe commonly used procedures for developing and sustaining a lifelong practice for engaging in contemplative prayer—*resting in God's presence and consenting to God's action*.

It cannot be overstressed that while these chapters are presented separately, there is a *oneness* to them in that there is a seamless transition from resting in God's presence to consenting to

Section Three: Building the Temple

God's action. Jerry Braza, retreat leader and author, captures this singleness and interconnectedness of meditation and daily living with the following story:

> A famous meditation teacher was once asked, "How long do you meditate each day?" The reply was, "Formally, for several hours per day I sit and meditate, and informally, I meditate all day long, with every activity becoming the focus of my meditation."[1]

The meditation session, with God's grace, helps to infuse the activities during the day with God's presence, which in turn enables us to rest more fully in God's presence during meditation. Contemplative prayer, in this way, becomes a way of life—*a path to union with God.*

---

1. Braza, *Practicing Mindfulness*, 39.

6

Establishing a Lifelong Practice of Prayer

Spiritual practice is not just sitting and meditation. Practice is looking, thinking, touching, drinking, eating and talking. Every act, every breath, and every step can be practice and can help us to become more ourselves.[1]

—THICH NHAT HANH

AT THE OUTSET, IT is most important to treat contemplative prayer as one part of our prayer life as we undertake our spiritual journey to union with God. That is, our contemplative prayer practice is best linked to, and supported by, other spiritual activities, such as: group prayer, church-based services, spiritual reading, service work, and other forms of individual prayer. In this way, there is more chance of experiencing a spiritual unity in our journey through the mutual benefits of each practice. It is helpful then to examine our prayer life to see what we have in place, what might be missing, and what may need enhancing.

---

1. Nhat Hanh, *Your True Home*, 151.

Section Three: Building the Temple

In addition, given we live in a very busy world with multiple demands on our time, it is also most important to attend to the many details involved in setting up and maintaining a contemplative prayer practice. Attending to these practical details helps to ensure that one's practice gets a reasonably strong start and is more likely to continue.

In this chapter, two broad guidelines are described for developing and sustaining a contemplative prayer practice: 1) Engaging in supportive spiritual practices, and 2) fidelity to the logistics of a practice.

Engaging in Supportive Spiritual Practices

Spiritual Activities

Several spiritual activities are usually available that may be included, or are already included, in our spiritual practice. William Shannon et al. noted that Thomas Merton, among other spiritual leaders, was a strong advocate of integrating other spiritual practices or services with a contemplative prayer practice:

> Merton stresses continually that there is no conflict between the public, communal prayer of the liturgy and personal and contemplative prayer . . . A contemplative appreciation of and participation in the mysterious transforming action of the liturgy will in turn provide the insight and impetus for authentic Christian action in the world.[2]

As with many practices, some activities may be helpful while others may not be a good fit. You are encouraged to experiment to find what works best for yourself and to modify the practices, where appropriate, to better meet your needs. The following practices and services, while not a complete list, are usually available:

---

2. Shannon et al., *Thomas Merton Encyclopedia*, 264.

Establishing a Lifelong Practice of Prayer

Church Services

Contemplative prayer practitioners are frequently affiliated with a church group that affords them the opportunity to become involved with an array of regular and seasonal spiritual practices such as: liturgies, Mass, Eucharist, sacraments, rosary, Taizé prayer, stations of the cross, and other special prayer services. Participants find that these services are another way to pray and to enhance their spiritual journey. In addition, you may find strength and spiritual support from other members—the community bonding effect.

Retreats

Residential retreats are available throughout the United States, where there are opportunities for extended contemplative prayer sessions in silence and stillness, typically held in relaxing settings. These retreats are usually facilitated in small groups by a trained retreat leader. Residential retreats can range in duration from weekends to several weeks. In addition, many facilities make available the option of private retreats. Quite often though, people are unable to take the time away from home or work to participate in residential retreats. One-day or half-day local retreats are frequently available and can accommodate the needs of those wanting longer periods for meditation but who cannot get away for residential retreats. Some practitioners try to participate in a residential retreat on an annual basis and, at others times, include a one-day or half-day retreat. The combination of a residential retreat and a local short retreat helps to strengthen your daily contemplative prayer practice over the year.

Regular Spiritual Reading

Taking a few minutes each day to do some quiet spiritual reading is a well-recognized way to augment your contemplative prayer practice. The mere act of stopping to engage in some reading has merit

Section Three: Building the Temple

in itself by helping to establish priorities, as well as developing the practice of disengaging from the busyness of life by becoming still. The content of what is read helps to add meaning to your spiritual journey, in addition to providing reminders of some particular aspect of your spiritual pathway that may need attention. It is usually best to reserve a set time and place for spiritual reading. This, of course, will vary from individual to individual. The key is to establish a routine so the spiritual reading becomes a *practice*. Another question is: How much time should be devoted to reading? Again, this will vary. Some practitioners prefer longer periods so they can experience the development of the content as in a book. Others prefer short, self-contained readings, such as daily reflections, thoughts for the day, and so on. Some practitioners like to make use of apps that are available and which vary in terms of subject matter, contributing authors, and material length. Regular spiritual reading can provide a richness to your spiritual path; however, it takes a solid commitment to develop a regular practice.

Classes

Another way to expand our knowledge base of the spiritual pathway, and to keep our contemplative prayer practice alive and stimulated, is to take part in classes. While the formality and requirements of classes may be off-putting to some, others appreciate the structure and guidance. Participants in classes often report that they read more, reflect more, and learn more than they otherwise would if left to their own resources. In addition, the experience of classes helps people to develop habits of spiritual reading and reflection that often carry over beyond the classes.

Perhaps one of the most exciting developments over the past decade or more has been the increased availability of online classes and webinars. The accessibility of courses online is a huge advantage to the busy person who can engage in classes in their own time and at their own pace. Moreover, there is an amazing array of content available in online coursework. Most people find that in their spiritual journey they are drawn to different topics at

Establishing a Lifelong Practice of Prayer

different times. As one practitioner shared, "I feel like a moving target when it comes to my spiritual interests and endeavors." The extensive range of courses available online can meet this ongoing and shifting need.

In addition, with the lockdown and social distancing requirements from COVID-19, there has been an emergence of Zoom meetings, classes, and dissemination opportunities. Practitioners find this technology to be a helpful way of keeping in touch with their friends and soul mates, as well as a source of information and ongoing training.

Spiritual Direction and Personal Support

Spiritual direction or pastoral counseling is a centuries-old practice, involving a one-to-one relationship with an experienced or trained professional. The object is to provide assistance and support to individuals as they deal with the ups and downs in their lifelong spiritual journey. The spiritual director is like a companion who carefully listens to the concerns, experiences, and challenges of individuals and helps them discern and respond to God's action in their lives. Practitioners typically find spiritual direction from trained professionals, clergy, and those experienced in pastoral care.

It is highly recommended that a person who may be interested in spiritual direction engage in a reasonably thorough search for a spiritual director. *Compatibility is particularly important.* Typically, a trial period is established, with an understanding such as, "Let's try this for a few weeks to see if it works out for us."

Sometimes people find support through a kindred soul, a fellow seeker. This experience is not the same as spiritual direction. Rather, it is more like two close friends getting together so that when mutual sharing occurs there is a kind of resonance that enriches and supports both parties in their spiritual journeys. John O'Donohue, Celtic scholar, describes this kind of kinship as *anam cara* (Gaelic

Section Three: Building the Temple

for "soul friend") that is: "A friend is a loved one who awakens your life in order to free the wild possibilities within you."[3]

Walking Meditation

Walking meditation is an ancient practice in Eastern religions that is becoming increasingly popular in the West. This practice dovetails very nicely with sitting meditation. As a friend lightly remarked, "In sitting meditation, I try to settle my body down. In walking meditation, I take it with me." The details suggested for sitting meditation, described in the next section, directly apply to walking meditation.

Practitioners report that walking meditation is most helpful as an activity between sitting meditation periods during longer sessions such as in retreats. Others find that a set walk in nature, such as walking along the river, on a trail through the woods, along the beach, or even just around the block, can be particularly prayerful. The key is to walk mindfully with the awareness that God is everywhere, and that each step in the walk connects us to God through his creation. The sense of stillness and silence, through the rhythmical steps of slow, mindful walking, becomes an experience of *oneness* with God in the universe—connecting with God through all of creation.

A more specific form of walking meditation that some seekers find helpful is to make use of *labyrinths*. Again, labyrinths have been around for thousands of years and can be found in a wide variety of settings: in churches and church grounds, prisons, town centers, beaches, parks, and other private and public centers. The circular design of labyrinths symbolizes, in a powerful manner, the spiritual journey of letting go, trusting the pathway, reaching the center, and returning to the exit. Labyrinth walks are typically available for group and individual practices. For those interested, labyrinths near you can be located at https://labyrinthlocator.com/.

---

3. O'Donohue, *Anam Cara*, 19.

Establishing a Lifelong Practice of Prayer

Service Work

Most Christians are familiar with the Martha and Mary story in Scripture[4], with Mary sitting still at Jesus' feet while Martha is busy preparing a meal in the kitchen. A dualistic interpretation is that love of Jesus can be expressed either in contemplative ways (sitting at Jesus' feet [Mary]), or in active ways (preparing a meal for Jesus [Martha]). However, a nondualisic interpretation is that the service of preparing a meal is *grounded* in the love of Jesus. That is, in following Jesus, we need to be like *both* Mary and Martha, engaging in *contemplative* and *service* activities.

There are endless opportunities to become involved with service activities in the community (especially in helping people with serious needs) such as volunteering at church and at community-based organizations (helping with meals, clothing, lodging, transport, etc.) or assisting neighbors, friends, and people in general with immediate needs. In this way, Jesus is acting through you to administer to the poor and needy, giving you opportunities to become one with God. These active services strengthen your contemplative prayer practice that, in turn, disposes us to become agents of God's love, especially for people in need.

Fidelity to the Logistics of a Practice

A second step for establishing and maintaining a contemplative prayer practice is to identify critical implementation details. These guidelines, or logistics, are based on common practices adopted by regular practitioners. The abiding suggestion is to understand that meditation is a very personal matter—a unique invitation from God to rest in his presence (chapter 7) and consent to his action (chapter 8). Therefore, it is most important to carefully examine these guidelines, and other practical details we may come across, to determine what works best for you. The following suggestions are commonly used practices that may be helpful to you in getting started or in reviewing your current practice.

4. Luke 10:38–42.

Section Three: Building the Temple

Meditating in a Group or Alone, or Both

An early decision that needs to be explored is whether to meditate with a group that has a regular meeting time and place or whether to meditate alone, usually at home. Group meditation brings a special energy which you don't experience when meditating alone. In addition, group meditations provide a regular structure that generates a special kind of bonding and camaraderie between members which helps to sustain attendance. Members look forward to seeing each other and chatting before and after the meeting. Meditating in a group also makes participants more aware of belonging to something larger than one's self.

It is most important to take steps to explore whether a particular group gathering is a good fit. It is strongly recommended to check out groups in your area and attend a meeting or two to discern whether or not a particular group will work for you.

Group meditation can be intimidating for a new person. It is helpful for newcomers to connect with a person who is a member of the group. Having a friend or contact at the meeting provides support and encouragement that can help to allay fears. The support person can share information on what to expect and can offer simple strategies for dealing with common difficulties and distractions such as: dealing with "monkey mind," restlessness, fidgeting, and the sense that time is dragging. In this way, newcomers better understand that these difficulties are quite normal. It is also particularly helpful, especially in the early stages, for the support person to meet with the newcomer after the meeting to debrief the experience.

Meditating alone is a preferred practice for many seekers. Moreover, meditating at home has become increasingly important, especially with the lockdowns and social distancing caused by the current COVID-19 pandemic. In addition, some people cannot attend group meetings because of health issues, transport difficulties, or other reasons. Practitioners typically find they need to use similar structures for meditating alone as for group meditations, such as: scheduling set times; designating a specific area of the home or outside location; using a set procedure for starting and finishing (an app, chimes, or music); and determining the frequency and duration of the meditation period.

Meditating alone is not necessarily inferior or superior to group meditation, nor do you need to choose one over the other. Many report that they practice *both* individual and group meditation, and that this combination serves them well.

Participating in Zoom Meetings

During these troubled times brought on by COVID-19, Zoom meetings have become very popular. These "virtual meetings" have emerged as a helpful way to connect church members with each other and with the various services. Zoom meetings have become a practical way of bringing people together for classes, services, meditation, business meetings, and social gatherings. While participants may miss the personal or direct contact with people, Zoom meetings provide a very convenient way to gather with others without the need to travel, and in a way that is safe. I fully expect Zoom meetings will continue in one form or another once COVID-19 has been contained.

Expressing Your Intention

A critical practice for beginning a meditation period is to simply and briefly express your *intention*. That is, to establish the mindset of accepting God's invitation to let go of all attachments and to rest in the divine presence and action, not only during the meditation period but throughout the day (see also chapters 7 and 8). Some practitioners use a set prayer while others prefer to use a word or phrase, as in centering prayer (described in chapter 2), that symbolizes their intention to become one with God during and following the meditation period. In addition, as you proceed in the meditation you can use this prayer, word, or phrase when distractions arise (and they surely will) to renew your intention and to gently bring yourself back to resting in God's presence and consenting to God's action.

It is also important to express your intention at the start of your session to help buttress against having the wrong intention. It is so easy to develop your own expectations for meditation, such as: seeking peace and serenity; finding solutions to problems; feeling good about the experience; and other self-serving outcomes. By expressly stating your intention, such as "Lord I wish to rest in your presence," or "God, I am grateful for the chance to be with you in heart and soul and mind," there is less chance for expectations of your *false self* to take over.

Tips for Establishing an Individual Practice

The following suggestions are commonly used steps for establishing and maintaining a meditation practice:

Time of day

Choose a time of day that is least likely to have interruptions. This could mean getting up earlier to conduct your practice first thing in the morning. Clearly, in today's busy world, you will probably need to have a backup time should the designated time become unavailable. Most people find it easier to meditate in the morning, while others find it beneficial to meditate in the evening as a way of letting go of aspects of the day and for showing gratitude for events of the day. It is often recommended to meditate twice a day, morning and evening, even just for short periods, if that is all that is available.

Location

Select a location in your home that is likely to be a quiet spot, where noise is minimized and silence maximized. Some people like to have a small shrine that becomes a sacred location for them,

Establishing a Lifelong Practice of Prayer

as well as a reminder to meditate. The key is to have a set area for your meditation so that when you enter this location you are already expressing your intention to sit in the presence of God.

Length

It is best to start out small, say five to ten minutes per session, and gradually lengthen the time to twenty to thirty minutes. By starting out small, there is less chance of making the session punishing or too challenging. It is always better, in terms of establishing a practice, to meditate short periods daily (ten minutes), versus a longer period once a week (forty minutes). The reason is that in meditating daily you are building a base that can be lengthened. In addition, you are providing more opportunities to be living in the presence of God both during and following the meditation period, which is the goal of the Christian journey.

How to start and end the session

Practitioners typically have a set way of starting and ending their contemplative prayer session. Common practices include using a timer, chimes, playing a DVD formatted with a designated time for meditation that opens and closes with some spiritual music, or using an app on a cell phone or device.

Physical set-up

It is worth giving thought to the physical set-up so as to create a quiet and reflective ambience for contemplative prayer, such as: dimming the lights, closing the blinds, lighting a candle, closing doors, and having a shrine.

Section Three: Building the Temple

Posture

It is most important to choose a physical posture that enables you to be both *comfortable* and *attentive*. Be aware of your physical limitations so that you can hold whatever posture you adopt without too much discomfort. I was reminded years ago by a retreat leader that meditation is not an endurance test. The decision on whether to use a kneeler, chair, cushion, or mat, or whether you are sitting, kneeling, or using a variation of a yoga posture, comes down to what works best for you. Initially, you might try different postures to determine the most suitable posture for yourself.

It is generally recommended to establish alignment between the head, spine, and hips, with special emphasis on having a straight spine. Shunryu Suzuki, Zen Master, recognized for helping to popularize Zen Buddhism in the United States, stressed the relationship between posture and attention when he wrote:

> The most important thing in taking the zazen [meditation] posture is to keep your spine straight . . . If you slump you will lose yourself. Your mind will be wandering about somewhere else.[5]

At the beginning of meditation, I like to rock from side to side a little and then stop in the center. This gives me a sense of squareness so that my hips, spine, and head are aligned as one unit. The overall key is to adopt a posture that you can comfortably hold for the duration of the session while maintaining a reasonable level of stillness and awareness.

Frequency

This decision refers to how often you meditate during the week. The ideal is to meditate daily; however, this level of practice may be too much initially. It may be more realistic to start out two or three times a week and build up to a daily practice. It is better to start out

---

5. Suzuki, *Zen Mind, Beginner's Mind*, 26–27.

small than try to begin with a daily practice and get discouraged and drop the practice.

Using technology

More and more practitioners utilize current technology to assist their practice. For example, there are many apps available, often for free, that can be used for guidance and tracking. In addition, with the restrictions regarding COVID-19, group meetings have been replaced by the widely adopted Zoom meetings.

In general, fidelity in following these details in your own way can help to establish and support a continued practice. The more you can establish a routine the more you are likely to sustain the practice.

Addressing Stillness and Silence

In chapter 4: "Necessity of Stillness and Silence," the importance of stillness and silence in your meditation practice was stressed. However, learning how to be *still* and *silent* can pose a definite challenge. Even when you choose a posture that enables you to settle your body and become still physically, you will likely find that the mind takes over, and soon you are flooded with thoughts, plans, feelings, and endless distractions—the mind is anything but still. Then when you get settled in a quiet area of your home, external distractions arise, like a chainsaw starting up or a dog barking. There are several commonly used strategies that you may find helpful in attaining a degree of stillness and silence in your practice.

Controlling breathing

Once your posture has been established, the next step is to focus on your breathing. It is evident that attention to breathing is a universal strategy which has been practiced during meditation in many religions for centuries. The focus on relaxed and even breathing

Section Three: Building the Temple

helps to settle down the body and establish a level of physical stillness. In addition, and perhaps more importantly, by concentrating on your breathing, you prevent the mind from taking over with all sorts of thoughts and emotions. The reason is simply that the mind can only concentrate on one thing at a time—in this case, your breathing.

Some people like to count their breaths as an aid to concentration on breathing. Personally, I find it helpful at the start of meditation to count my breaths up to ten and then start again. The reason is that it is easy to count subconsciously and then be thinking of something else. Initially, I found I was up to a count of thirty to forty while thinking about the rest of my morning! However, by starting over after a count of ten, I had to concentrate more on counting my breaths. Counting your breaths also serves as a particularly helpful tool when distractions arise. Once you become aware of a distraction, simply start counting your breaths and resume the focus of breathing in an even and relaxed manner.

Controlling breathing can also be helpful in the practice of walking meditation. One strategy is to connect your breathing with your steps. For example, breathe in (one step), breathe out (next step), and so on. In this way a comfortable rhythm can be established that leads to a sense of oneness with body, walking, ground, and universe.

Addressing unwelcome noise

Coupled with the need for stillness of body and mind is the importance of establishing *silence*. Silence, however, does not mean an absence of noise, as you cannot live in that kind of bubble. You can, though, choose a setting where noise is minimized and silence maximized. Moreover, silence in meditation really means *silence of the mind*, so that when some noise occurs, we *accept* it as a necessary part of our environment, as *part of the deal*. Noise becomes a distraction when you allow it. I am reminded of a friend who told me once that "I learned to meditate in a subway in New York City."

Establishing a Lifelong Practice of Prayer

His point was he had to accept that noise was a given part of his meditation environment.

Most find it impossible and counterproductive to try to block out noise, especially sustained noise. The mere fact of trying to suppress the awareness of noise, and to be unsuccessful, can cause agitation, perhaps resentment, that can easily disrupt your interior silence and stillness. Once again, concentrating on your breath can be a useful tool for dealing with sudden or sustained noise. That is, to treat the noise as a distraction, just like thoughts, and return to counting your breaths.

Using a sacred word or phrase

The late Fr. Thomas Keating and others have undertaken monumental steps in recent years to bring the practice of contemplative prayer to everyday Christians. They have developed teachings and practices called *centering prayer* (described briefly in chapter 2) to enable Christians to engage fruitfully in the kind of contemplative prayer that has often been regarded as the domain of monastics, mystics, and desert fathers and mothers. One practice in centering prayer that has been widely adopted for establishing stillness and silence is the use of a sacred word or phrase.

This sacred word or phrase is uttered prayerfully at the beginning of your meditation to represent your intention to rest in the presence and action of God. The sacred word or phrase is typically simple and brief, such as "Jesus," "My God," or "Here I am, Lord." Again, the chosen sacred word or phrase is not meant to be a subject for reflection. Rather, it is a humble act of faith in expressing your desire to be open to God's presence and action.

You may find it helpful to link the sacred word or phrase to your breath. For example, if the sacred word or phrase is "Jesus," a two-syllable word, on the in-breath the first syllable, "Jes-," is uttered silently, and on the out-breath the second syllable, "-us," is uttered. Similarly, a phrase can be broken up into two parts. For example, "Here I am, Lord," can be divided as "Here I am" for the in-breath and "Lord" with the out-breath.

Section Three: Building the Temple

A practice I like to use is to begin the meditation with just counting my breaths, then link my breath to a sacred word, "Jesus," and then let the sacred word fade away to using no words and just resting in and being open to the presence and action of God (subject matter for the next two chapters). You can also use your sacred word as a way to address distractions, whether they are external (such as noise), or internal (such as thoughts and emotions). When the distractions arise, you gently, slowly, and silently utter your sacred word or phrase to reestablish your focus and intention.

Controlling your eyes

Unless you are careful, your eyes can set the occasion for distractions and disruption during contemplative prayer. Obviously, if you are looking around to see who is coming in late, or looking up to see where a noise is coming from, you have moved away from your focus of resting in God's presence. The challenge is that looking around, or letting your eyes engage with something, is for the most part *reflexive*. To buttress against this reactive looking, it is best to close your eyes or cast them downwards. I prefer casting my eyes downward (as you often see in statues of the Buddha). The reason is that I tend to doze off if I close my eyes as I use the very same steps to still the body and mind in bed for sleeping that I use for beginning meditation. Again, select what works best for you. The intent, by closing your eyes or casting them down, is to minimize distraction to help attain stillness and silence.

Some practitioners like to use what is called "soft eyes." That is, they pick a spot or object low down, usually on the floor, and look at it not in a direct or fixed way, but rather as a vacant glance where they are also aware of objects in their peripheral vision. This strategy can not only can help to settle down the mind and body, but can also be used to address persistent or strong distractions. The strategy called *peripheral scanning* involves looking at this spot; then, without moving your eyes or head, allowing yourself to see objects in your peripheral vision and slowly allowing your vision to scan outwards taking in objects; and then allowing your

Establishing a Lifelong Practice of Prayer

vision to slowly move back to the initial spot on the floor. The key is to maintain looking at the spot on the floor with soft eyes and to become aware of objects in the range of your peripheral vision—*peripheral scanning*. Practitioners report that this strategy is a powerful way to deal with strong distractions. Typically, peripheral scanning is used two or three times and then followed by counting breaths or using one's sacred word or phrase.

Managing physical discomfort

One experience common to everyone who meditates is the "troublesome itch" or physical aches. Normally, we address these physical aggravations or distractions by making some sort of movements such as scratching or changing positions. We also understand that movement, especially constant movement, can be disruptive to contemplative prayer, not only for yourself, but also for your neighbor. Constant moving negates the experience of stillness. It is helpful to have a strategy to deal with these physical discomforts. The first recommended step is to ignore the physical discomfort; that is to simply tough it out and avoid, at all costs, immediately responding to the concern. Simply treat it as a distraction. If the problem persists, treat it in the same way as mental distractions (thoughts and emotions) by returning to counting your breaths or your sacred word or phrase. Some find it helpful to connect the breathing to the problem. For example, breathe in on one count and breathe out on the next count, visualizing the breath going through the itch or the ache. In this way as the breath is released, the itch or ache may be released. However, if the problem still persists, deal with it directly by scratching or moving. The overall recommendation is to *delay* responding directly to the physical distractions.

The practice of contemplative prayer is not something that will happen by itself or by chance. Rather we need to take measured steps, and with the help of God's grace, we can establish a regular practice. Many practitioners find involvement with other prayer forms, such as church-based services, and spiritual

Section Three: Building the Temple

practices (reflective reading, for example) can enhance and support a regular contemplative prayer practice. In addition, as in forming any good habit, we also need to pay particular attention to several proven practical logistics for developing and sustaining a contemplative prayer practice.

For Personal Application

1. What other prayer forms and spiritual activities do you engage in that may support your meditation practice? What might be added?
2. Do you prefer to meditate in a group, alone, or both?
3. How do you express your intention at the start of your meditation?
4. What details or logistics involved in setting up your practice are already in place, and what might need to be modified or added?
5. How do you establish stillness and silence?
6. How do you address distractions?

> **Action Response:** Is there something *specific* in this chapter that draws you to make a change in, or add to, your spiritual journey?

7

Contemplative Prayer
Resting in God's Presence

*My God, I pray better to You by breathing,
I pray better to You by walking than by talking.*[1]

—THOMAS MERTON

CONTEMPLATIVE PRAYER IS OFTEN described in terms of what it is not, defined by *negation*. For example, we read that contemplative prayer is nonthinking, objectless, and wordless. Yet, these are the very tools or actions we typically engage in when we pray at church, whether in groups or by ourselves! We are forced to ask, "If these actions are taken away, what are we left with when we pray? Nothing?" The contemplative prayer teacher would answer by saying, "Now you're catching on." Fortunately, we have received strong encouragement, examples, and helpful information from the saints, spiritual writers, and practitioners that contemplative prayer is an extraordinary gift from God that is there waiting for us.

---

1. Merton, *Dialogues with Silence*. 57.

Section Three: Building the Temple

There are two highly interrelated essential dimensions to contemplative prayer frequently alluded to throughout this book that will now be more fully described:

- Resting in the presence of God (chapter 7)
- Consenting to God's action (chapter 8)

In this chapter information and suggestions are offered for understanding and establishing the practice of contemplative prayer, of resting in God's presence without thinking and without words. Topics addressed include: 1) The challenging dynamic of my action and God's action, 2) limitations of the word "contemplation," 3) understanding resting in the presence and action of God, 4) describing the experience of contemplative prayer without words, and 5) inherent challenges.

The Challenging Dynamic of My Action and God's Action

One of the biggest challenges we face in establishing a contemplative prayer practice is to have some understanding of the relationship between my action and God's action. In a somewhat light-hearted manner, this relationship was brought home to me by an exchange with a former Archbishop of Canterbury reported by Carmelite priest and theologian Ernest Larkin:

> A story appearing in the London Tablet some years ago helps locate the essence of prayer. The Archbishop of Canterbury at the time was being interviewed on television and he was asked about his prayer. "Do you pray?" was the question. "Yes," he answered, "I pray each day." "And how much do you pray?" He answered: "About a minute." There was surprise on the interviewer's face, so the Archbishop added: "Of course, it takes me about 29 minutes to get to that one minute.[2]

---

2. Larkin, "Contemplative Prayer," 99.

Contemplative Prayer

The point made, as I understand it, is that contemplative prayer refers to those moments, however brief or passing, when God's presence prevails. Our actions in this sense are limited to getting ourselves ready to be open and receptive to God's presence when and however it may appear.

In a similar vein, Martin Laird describes the relationship between our effort in prayer and God's action in this way:

> A spiritual practice simply disposes us to allow something to take place. For example, a gardener does not actually grow plants. A gardener practices certain gardening skills that facilitate growth that is beyond the gardener's direct control.[3]

It is also important to realize that in contemplative prayer the relationship between our action and God's action is not simply *linear* or *temporal*. That is, we don't do what we can to get ready for God's action as in phase one, and then remain resting in God's presence and consenting to God's action, as in phase two. The dynamic is more like cell phone reception in remote areas where we find intermittent connectivity—sometimes we are connected, then we lose it, then we are connected again, and so on. In effect, there is a constant back and forth in being connected and losing connection.

Similarly, during contemplative prayer, we typically find that our thoughts come and go, sometimes quite frequently, and other times less frequently. While we cannot control the thoughts from coming, we can learn to give them *less attention*. It is as if we don't have to directly attend to the distraction, to "watch the movie" or "add to the script," so to speak. In this way, we will find moments between thoughts, often referred to as "the gap," where there is a sacred silence for us to rest in God's presence and action. These moments, however brief and fleeting, are the heart of contemplative prayer. Many of us have taken encouragement by the reported exchange between a Sister and retreat leader Thomas Keating, following a centering prayer session. The Sister said, "I am a failure,

---

3. Laird, *Into the Silent Land*, 3–4.

Section Three: Building the Temple

I must have been distracted a thousand times." Keating replied, "How wonderful!! A thousand opportunities to return to God."[4]

Contemplative prayer, then, can be seen as those moments of interior silence where we rest in the presence of God—those sacred moments between our distractions. We should not be discouraged if our thoughts are present more than we'd like. Our challenge is to do the best we can to set the occasion for God's gift of contemplative prayer to be given to us and, as we become aware of distractions, to gently bring our mind back to our center—God.

Limitations of the Word "Contemplation"

I am reminded of a line my high school English teacher often used: "The best way to ruin a good idea is to write it down." His message was, as I understood it then, that words themselves are limited in meaning. So the words we use to describe an idea or experience do not fully capture what we are wanting to say. The words fall short and weaken the idea we are trying to express. The same can certainly be said of the word *contemplation* when it is used to describe the prayer form of resting in the presence of God. The reason is because "contemplation" is a derivative of the Latin word *contemplatio*, which literally means "act of looking at." In other words, contemplation is tied to an *object*—something that can be looked at. For example, we experience contemplation when we look at something with marked attention, such as a painting, beautiful scenery, a landscape, and so on. Contemplation, in this sense, is tied to the relationship between subject and object. That is, *we* (subject) contemplate some *thing* (object). In other words, contemplation denotes separation or dualism. However, in contemplative prayer, the ideal is the *direct opposite*—nondualism where there is no separation between the subject, *we*, and the object, *God*. Rather, we are drawn into God, by God, to become *one* with God. There is no subject/object relationship—rather a profound *oneness*. Therefore, when we use the word "contemplation" in the

---

4. Bourgeault, "Method," para. 3.

Contemplative Prayer

context of contemplative prayer, it is important to understand that it means becoming one with God where God is neither subject nor object. Jesus often refers to this oneness in his teachings, such as: "I am the vine, you are the branches,"[5] and "I will not leave you orphaned... On that day you will know that I am in my Father and you in me, and I in you."[6]

Contemplative prayer has often been referred to as "objectless prayer." For example, Willigis Jager, German Benedictine monk and teacher, wrote, "Christian mystical writers use the word *contemplation* in reference to a specific kind of objectless prayer."[7] Similarly, Cynthia Bourgeault uses the term "objectless awareness"[8] to describe the desired state of openness and receptivity when we engage in contemplative prayer.

Understanding Resting in God's Presence

I realize it is a challenge to establish a regular routine and have to deal with the incessant thoughts and feelings that emerge during contemplative prayer. Now, we examine an additional challenge that is more elusive and intangible—the practice of resting in the presence of God without words. At this juncture, it is absolutely essential that we constantly remind ourselves that prayer is a gift from God (noted in chapter 2).

We can gain some understanding of what it means to rest in the presence of God without words by examining several different human experiences. These experiences capture how we can become immersed in a situation, *to rest in it without words.*

---

5. John 15:5.
6. John 14:18, 20.
7. Jager, *Contemplation*, 85 (emphasis original).
8. Bourgeault, *Heart of Centering Prayer*, 129.

Section Three: Building the Temple

Child Coming to Sit with His Mother

I was trying to explain what it meant to rest in the presence of God during a retreat and one of the participants shared this comment as I recall it:

> That brings back a treasured memory of my son when he was about four years old. He would come into the living room when I was reading on the sofa and he would just sit beside me. He wouldn't say anything and was content to just sit there and snuggle. I remember how very special it was for me. I felt no need at all to say anything to him and was perfectly content to sit there with him in silence. Then he would get up and go off to something else.

This example illustrates that both the mom and son were very comfortable in each other's presence, were communicating with each other, and that there was no need to say anything—they rested in each other's presence without words.

Absorption in Life Experiences

We can readily recall events in our lives where we are fully captivated by something and experience a sense of awe, oneness, silence, and the sense of resting in it without the need for words. For example:

- sitting in front of a fire
- watching waves rolling in at the coast
- walking through a sunlit forest
- gazing at a vast canyon
- holding a newborn child
- listening to some meaningful music
- relaxing in a chair in a still and quiet space as the sun sets

These examples bring a sense of *immersion*, becoming one with the experience of the moment to the point where words are certainly unnecessary. There is the sense of resting in the situation. This sense of oneness in these experiences was captured in a most poignant manner by minister and educator Howard Thurman when he wrote:

> As a boy in Florida, I walked along the beach of the Atlantic in the quiet stillness that can only be completely felt when the murmur of the ocean is stilled, and the tides move stealthily along the shore. I held my breath against the night and watched the stars etch their brightness on the face of the darkened canopy of the heavens. I had the sense that all things, the sand, the sea, the stars, the night, and I were one lung through which all of life breathed. Not only was I aware of a vast rhythm enveloping all, but I was a part of it and it was a part of me.[9]

Becoming One with God

Another challenge in contemplative prayer as we rest in the presence of God is to gain some understanding of what it means to become one with God. Do we become God? Are we the same as God, meaning is there no difference between God and us? These questions seem to border on being heretical. Yet, we are frequently reminded of the divine indwelling and the call to oneness with God throughout Scripture: "Jesus answered him, 'Those who love me will keep my word, and my Father will love them, and we will come to them and make our home in them.'"[10] Similarly, St. Paul proclaimed, "It is no longer I who live, but it is Christ who lives in me."[11]

Franz Jalics, Jesuit priest and theologian, offers a simple analogy for helping us to understand this elusive teaching that we are called to be one with God and yet we are still ourselves in God. He describes a conversation with a tree:

> Just imagine that we are standing in front of a mighty tree with huge branches. If I asked one of the branches,

9. Thurman, *With Head and Heart*, 225–26.
10. John 14:23.
11. Gal 2:20.

Section Three: Building the Temple

> "Are you branch or are you tree?" it would have to answer, "I am branch and I am tree and I am one." If I went on asking, "What makes you think that you are a tree?" it would have to answer that it knows this through the life energy that passes through it, because it is at the same time the life energy of the tree as well as of the branch ... Look closely at the force flowing though you and then follow it up to the very source, where the force is no longer branch, but tree. That is how it will dawn on you, that you are all one with the tree.[12]

A helpful analogy for me in addressing this paradox of being one with God and yet separate is what artists call linear perspective. That is, where parallel lines appear to converge in the distance at a vanishing point on the horizon line. All of us at some point have experienced this illusion by standing in the middle of a railway line, or a long straight path. When we look to either side, we see that the railway lines or edges of the path are clearly parallel and separate from each other. However, as we look into the distance these lines and edges converge to a single point. In this sense the lines are separate at first glance, but when we look into the distance, they converge to become one. In a similar manner, while we see ourselves as separate from God, yet when we look beyond, with the eyes of faith, we become one with God.

In our spiritual journey, we are called to become one in God. There is a oneness, with God through his indwelling, that becomes available to us through the grace of God in our contemplative prayer. Our challenge, with God's grace, is to be open, receptive, and responsive to this gift.

Spending Time with Loved One or Friend

Most of us have experienced a difference in spending time with a loved one or intimate friend compared to being with someone less well known. One difference is the comfort level when there are gaps in the conversation—when there is *silence*. With the friend

12. Jalics, *Contemplative Way*, 42.

Contemplative Prayer

or loved one there is no need to be talking all the time, and there is a comfort level when silence arises. There is a certain level of relaxation in each other's company that does not require words to be spoken all the time. However, with someone less known there is more of a need to be talking all the time. So that when there is silence, there is a level of discomfort or even tension. In these cases, the comfort level is best when there are no gaps in the conversation. By contrast, the comfort level between loved ones or friends is much the same whether there is conversation or gaps in the conversation.

In a similar vein, I am also reminded of weddings where there are usually lots of words and rituals but there is one special moment of silence when the officiant traditionally says: "You may now kiss the bride." In this moment, the bride and groom gaze at each other *before* they kiss—no words are spoken, no words need to be spoken. There is simply a powerful moment of resting in each other's love without words.

Typically in contemplative prayer we strive to let go of our thoughts and feelings and enter a silence, a *wordless* phase. We simply assume a position of waiting, trusting, and gently gazing in the presence and action of the divine indwelling.

Saying Goodbye to a Loved One or Dear Friend

In a similar manner, another common experience is the silence when we are saying goodbye to a loved one or close friend. The experience is more telling when we are not sure if and when we will see the person again. We have often seen portrayals of such scenes in movies and in literature when words are absent at farewells where loved ones are heading off to war or departing for unknown lengths of time. Also, when parties have shared in-depth, intense, and life-changing experiences, they struggle to find words when it is departure time. For example, Peter Matthiessen, renowned naturalist, environmental activist, and author, in his classic book *The Snow Leopard*, speaks to this situation. He had just finished a two-month grueling trek in the Himalayas with his zoologist

Section Three: Building the Temple

friend George Schaller and had this to say when it was time for the two of them to say goodbye:

> I try to express inexpressible thanks as we shake hands. "I've been very very *moved* . . ." I say, and stop. Such words are only clutter, they do not say what I mean. I am moved from where I used to be, and can never go back.[13]

It is noteworthy that Matthiessen could not only not find the right words, but he also felt that words got in the way, were *clutter*.

Describing the Experience of Contemplative Prayer without Words

This particular section on trying to describe the experience of resting in God's presence without words is one of the most elusive parts of this book. Not only is it challenging to find the right words to adequately capture the experience, but the experience itself, for most of us, is quite shadowy, unpredictable, and inconstant. I have found it helpful to reflect on descriptions by saints, spiritual writers, and practitioners who in their own way have found meaningful words. My suggestion is to take some time to read these descriptions prayerfully with a particular focus on expressions that capture the meaning of *resting in* the presence of God where there is an emphasis on *wordlessness* and *silence*. Hopefully, in this way, you may further your understanding of contemplative prayer and experience some encouragement to persevere with the practice.

Villager (reported in Albert Haase)

> St Jean Vianney, parish priest of French town Ars, noticed a villager who visited the church often, asked him one day during a visit what he said to God during his visits. The

---

13. Matthiesson, *Snow Leopard*, 271 (emphasis original).

man answered, "Oh I don't say anything to God, Monsieur le Cure. I look at God and God looks at me."[14]

St. Mother Teresa of Calcutta

There is a story of a conversation Mother Teresa had with an inquirer when asked about her prayer life:

The inquirer apparently asked, as perhaps we would ask, if we had the same opportunity: "When you pray, what do you say to God?"

Mother Teresa's reply was quite simple and stark: "I don't talk. I only listen."

The inquirer then asked:

"Then what is it that God says to you?"

Mother Teresa smiled, looked at the ground and said: "God doesn't talk either. God also listens."[15]

Thomas Merton

Prayer is not reasoning, it is intuitive, relaxed, letting go of, collapsing into God.[16]

Simply speaking, I have a very simple way of prayer. It is centered entirely on the presence of God . . . Such is my ordinary way of prayer. It is not thinking about anything but a direct seeing of the face of the invisible which cannot be found unless we become lost in Him who is invisible.[17]

---

14. Villager, as quoted in Haase, *Coming Home*, 89.
15. St. Mother Teresa of Calcutta, "How They Prayed," 162.
16. Merton, *Hidden in the Same Mystery*, 58.
17. Merton, "Letter to Abdul Haziz," 62–64.

Section Three: Building the Temple

Simone Weil

Absolute unmixed attention is prayer.[18]

Thomas Keating

The root of all prayer is silence ... It is the opening of the mind and heart, body, and emotions, our whole being—to God, the Ultimate Mystery, beyond words, thoughts and emotions.[19]

Cynthia Bourgeault

Somewhere in those depths of silence I came upon my first experiences of God as a loving presence that was always near, and prayer as a simple trust in that presence.[20]

St. John of the Cross

For contemplation is naught else than a secret, peaceful and loving infusion from God, which, if it be permitted, enkindles the soul with the spirit of love.[21]

Julian of Norwich

The fullness of joy is to behold God in everything.[22]

---

18. Weil, *Gravity and Grace*, 117.
19. Keating, *Open Mind, Open Heart*, 12.
20. Bourgeault, *Centering Prayer*, 5.
21. St. John of the Cross, *Dark Night of the Soul*, 34.
22. Julian of Norwich, *Revelation of Love*, 68.

Contemplative Prayer

Carl McColman

> Beholding, in the mystical sense, is so much more than mere seeing or looking. It involves gazing, loving, receiving love, a sense of mutuality. We behold God in response to God beholding us.[23]

St. Therese of Lisieux

> Shortly before she died at age twenty-four, Therese of Lisieux lay in the convent infirmary, unable to sleep. Her older sister, Celine, also a nun in the convent, looked in on her and asked her what she was doing.
> "I am praying," Therese responded.
> "And what are you saying to God?" her sister asked.
> "I am saying nothing. I am loving him," Therese replied.[24]

Even though we have prayerfully read these citations and related readings we may still feel strongly challenged to understand what it means exactly to rest in the presence of God. We need to remind ourselves constantly that all prayer, contemplative prayer in this case, is a *gift from God*, an invitation to become one with God at the center of our being. While some understanding can be helpful, the bottom line is that our practice of prayer is a response in faith and trust to a call from God.

Inherent Challenges

It is safe to say that once you begin to meditate on a regular basis, it is only a matter of time before difficulties arise. It is as if the honeymoon is over. It is worth spending a little time examining some of the common challenges you are likely to face as you develop and try to sustain a contemplative prayer practice. By so doing,

---

23. McColman, *Answering the Contemplative Call*, 97.
24. St. Therese of Lisieux, as quoted in Haase, *Coming Home*, 89

we may better understand what is involved and see these apparent roadblocks as graced opportunities for spiritual growth.

The Experience of Darkness, Boredom, or Dryness

Spiritual writers consistently warn that when you open yourself in meditation, surrender to God's will, and assent to God's action, you will likely experience a profound void characterized by periods of darkness, uncertainty, or confusion. These writers explain that such experiences, described by St. John of the Cross as *the dark night of the soul*, are a necessary part of the spiritual journey. For example, Mother Teresa, canonized by the Catholic church in 2016, struggled for many years with these kinds of challenging doubts as she wrote:

> In my soul I feel just that terrible pain of loss, of God not wanting me—of God not being God—of God not existing.[25]

Similarly, Thomas Merton widely recognized for his commitment to the contemplative life, wrote:

> Before the spirit can see the living God, it must be blind even to the highest perceptions and judgment of its natural intelligence. It must enter into pure darkness. But this darkness is pure light—because it is the infinite Light of God Himself. And the mere fact that His Light is infinite means that it is darkness to our finite minds.[26]

The message is that darkness, confusion, and emptiness are part-and-parcel of the experience of contemplative prayer that requires us to fully trust that God will lead us from this darkness to the light of *divine presence* at some point. The basic exhortation is *to stay the course*.

Unfortunately, some participants misinterpret this state of emptiness or dryness as a sign that meditation is not for them.

---

25. St. Mother Teresa of Calcutta, "How They Prayed," 163.
26. Merton, *Ascent to Truth*, 50.

Contemplative Prayer

Group leaders and seasoned practitioners are strongly encouraged to inform those trying to establish a meditation practice, especially when starting out, to *expect* a level of boredom or dryness as they develop their practice. The best advice for them is to stay with it, endure the period of dryness as an integral part of the spiritual journey, and remain steadfast in the practice.

Coming Face to Face with Your False Self

Practitioners often report that consistently spending time in meditation gives them a clearer picture of who they are. The process of letting go and letting be brings to the surface what is important to them, what character issues they may have, and similar insights about themselves, both positive and negative. This closer contact with reality can heighten their awareness of troubling aspects in their lives and personal struggles such as:

- recovering from addictions (alcohol, drugs, video gaming, gambling, pornography)
- habitual problematic behavior (temper outbursts, violence, compulsive stealing, chronic lying)
- personal flaws or character defects that cause lack of trust in one's self (always blaming others, holding resentments).

In some cases, when meditation brings individuals closer to these troublesome issues, discomfort can arise, causing them to abandon their practice. They struggle to accept the real core of their being, their *true self*, is made in the image and likeness of God, and that God's gift of deep healing is available to them regardless of their history. Rather, they see their core as seriously flawed and not really redeemable or worthy of God's graces.

While there are no short-cuts to help those afflicted in these ways, the key is to continually remind ourselves of the core belief that *you*, along with everyone else, are created in the *image and likeness of God*. God's steadfast love is always present, regardless of the contours of your life journey. The key suggestion is to remain

Section Three: Building the Temple

resolute in your practice, trust in God's healing love, and believe that, with God's grace, the ability to embrace your true self will grow over time. However, to be on the safe side, if individuals are significantly disturbed by what they are facing, they should seek additional support from a spiritual director, meditation leader, or professional counselor.

Beware of Setting Expectations—Make Room for God

One of the biggest impediments to developing a regular practice in meditation is our need to *set expectations*. Unfortunately, the human predisposition to take charge may lead us to seek control and feel responsible for what happens during and following meditation. When these expectations are not met, we may conclude that we are doing something wrong and seek other methods. Or we may determine that meditation is "not for me."

Again, we need to continually remind ourselves that contemplative prayer is a *gift from God*—an invitation to become one with God at the center of our being. Our role then is to rest in the divine presence and to be open, receptive, and responsive to whatever we may feel drawn to during or following our meditation. We are invited to step aside—*to make room for God!* Or, as Ed Cyzewski, author and spiritual leader on contemplation, expresses so simply, "Contemplative prayer removes us from the driver's seat."[27] When we sense that we are still in the driver's seat, it is important to go back to our *intention* for engaging in contemplative prayer by reciting our sacred word or prayer (see chapter 6 for further details in the section "Expressing Our Intention").

It is also critical that we do not *judge* or *evaluate* our meditation. Such judgment is futile because we can evaluate a meditation only in terms of our own expectations, which are counterproductive to letting go and resting in the presence and action of God.

This chapter addresses an essential aspect of contemplative prayer in terms of *resting in the presence of God* without words.

---

27. Cyzewski, "*Flee, Be Silent, Pray* Quotes," para. 6.

Contemplative Prayer

While the description looks relatively simple, the experience of contemplative prayer is particularly challenging. Part of the difficulty has to do with this form of prayer having an emphasis on *being* rather than *doing*. We typically find it much easier to describe our experiences related to *doing* compared to *being*. However, we have the assurance from Scripture, church teachings, and spiritual writings, that contemplative prayer is an extraordinary gift from God and that we are strongly encouraged to do what we can, with trust in God's steadfast love, to develop and sustain a practice of this form of prayer.

For Personal Application

1. What does it mean to you to rest in the presence of God?
2. What experiences have you had where you felt captivated when contemplating something?
3. What experiences have you had where words were not necessary?
4. Do any of the cited examples of resting in God's presence appeal to you?
5. What factors inhibit your meditation practice and what do you do about it?

> **Action Response**: Is there something *specific* in this chapter that draws you to make a change in, or add to, your spiritual journey?

8

Contemplative Prayer

Consenting to God's Action

Contemplative prayer as a special gift from God is one that has been given. The proper response to this gift is to consent to God's presence and action manifested in us by the desire for God.[1]

—THOMAS KEATING

CONTEMPLATIVE PRAYER CAN BE described in terms of two closely interrelated and essential facets—*resting in the presence of God* and *consenting to God's action*. To help our understanding, these two elements are usually addressed as separate entities when in fact they are not. Elizabeth O'Connor, in her particularly helpful analysis, writes of the need for a balance between seeking God dwelling within, and in seeking God dwelling among us in the world:

> "Inward journey" and "outward journey" are familiar terms in our community. We use them to describe what the Christian life is all about. We use them to describe the meaning of membership in the church of the Saviour.

---

1. Keating, *Consenting to God*, 5–6.

Contemplative Prayer

> As a commentary of faith, we are committed to being on an inward journey and a people on an outward journey.[2]

In other words, God's presence and God's action can be found both within ourselves and in our world. In practice God's presence and God's action cannot be separated.

Unfortunately, one of the biggest limitations of our intellect is that we seem to understand things better when they are separated. We have a strong penchant for making discriminations (dualism) rather than seeing inherent oneness and unity (nondualism). It is hoped, though, that once some common ground is understood, at least to some extent, our contemplative prayer practice will reflect a unity and reciprocity between the presence and action of God within ourselves and within the world. Given this, I addressed one central dimension of contemplative prayer, *resting in the presence of God*, in chapter 7. The purpose of the current chapter is to describe the practice of the other critical dimension—*consenting to God's action*. Topics addressed are: 1) Guidance from Scripture and spiritual leaders, 2) being open, receptive, and responsive to God's will, 3) apparent conflict between God's will and my will, 4) consenting to God's will in a busy life, 5) responding to God's call by participating in God's action, 6) discerning God's will, and 7) living with uncertainty.

Guidance from Scripture and Christian Leaders

Once we examine Scripture and the writings of Christian leaders, we see constant appeals to align our wills with the calls from God. These citations have been selected to provide you with the opportunity to sit quietly and reflect on God's actions and our response on our spiritual journey.

---

2. O'Connor, *Journey Inward, Journey Outward*, 10.

Section Three: Building the Temple

Scripture

Trust in the Lord with all your heart, and do not rely on your own insight. In all your ways acknowledge him, and he will make straight your paths.[3]

Take delight in the Lord, and he will give you the desires of your heart. Commit your way to the Lord; trust in him, and he will act.[4]

Whoever does the will of God is my brother and sister and mother.[5]

Your kingdom come. Your will be done, on earth as it is in heaven.[6]

Anyone who resolves to do the will of God will know whether the teaching is from God or whether I am speaking on my own.[7]

Christian Leaders

Thomas Merton

There is something left in the depths of our being which is this yes to God . . . If we reflect and think, we sense that the whole meaning of our life consists in this yes to God.[8]

---

3. Prov 3:5–6.
4. Ps 37:4–5.
5. Mark 3:35.
6. Matt 6:10.
7. John 7:17.
8. Merton, *Springs of Contemplation*, 262.

Contemplative Prayer

Beatrice Bruteau

God is the author of all that is. Everything starts in and with God whose action and love are never determined or elicited by anything in the environment.[9]

Dietrich Bonhoeffer

Who stands fast? Only the man whose final standard is not his reason, his principles, his conscience, his freedom, or his virtue, but who is ready to sacrifice all this when he is called to obedient and responsible action in faith and in exclusive allegiance to God—the responsible man, who tries to make his whole life an answer to the question and call of God.[10]

Evelyn Underhill

Our contemplation and our action, our humble self-opening to God, keeping ourselves sensitive to His music and light, and our generous self-opening to our fellow creatures, keeping ourselves sensitive to their needs, ought to form one life; mediating between God and His world, and bringing the saving power of the Eternal into time.[11]

Jean-Pierre de Caussade

When the will of God has been made known to us and we, in turn, make it plain that we are only too glad to abandon ourselves to it, we shall be given most powerful help. We shall then know the joy of God's arrival in

---

9. Bruteau, *Radical Optimism*, 81.
10. Bonhoeffer, *Letters and Papers from Prison*, 4.
11. Underhill, *Spiritual Life*, 98.

us and savor it more intensely the more completely we abandon ourselves to his adorable will.[12]

Being Open, Receptive, and Responsive to God's Will

Throughout this book, contemplative prayer has been described in terms of resting in God's presence and consenting to God's action. It is one thing to rest in God's presence, but what does it mean to rest in God's action? This question is usually explained in terms of following God's will or taking whatever action is needed to undertake and sustain our spiritual journey in Christ. The next question becomes, "How does this apply to contemplative prayer?" Some have found that the analogy of getting started with reading a new book can shed some light on a possible answer. Specifically, when we begin to read a new book, we try to create a readiness in ourselves to receive the information in the book as it is intended. We want to avail ourselves to what is written and to allow ourselves to be taken wherever the book may lead us. We say it is a good book when it takes us to new territory in an engaging way, or perhaps, validates what we already know or believe. In effect, to ready ourselves for a new book we try to put ourselves in a position to be *open* and *receptive* to what is written and *allow* ourselves to be drawn to wherever the book may take us.

The same is true in contemplative prayer. We enter the prayer with the intention of being *open, receptive,* and *responsive* to God's presence and action, and commit to follow, as best we can, whatever we may be called to do during the prayer or during the day.

The Apparent Conflict between God's Will and My Will

It is quite clear that to live a full Christian life we must draw on, and single-mindedly live, the message from Scripture, to align

---

12. Caussade, *Abandonment to Divine Providence*, 41–42.

our will with God's will. Moreover, consenting to God's action is an integral part of contemplative prayer. This commitment can pose a significant challenge to many seekers as there is something daunting and seemingly unnatural about abandoning our will. We spend so much of our day exercising our will as we do in trying to take charge of our lives, making decisions, and being responsible and accountable. Consequently, the practice of abandoning or surrendering our will is somewhat unnerving and appears to go against the way we operate at work, with our family, and by ourselves. However, Christians are quite familiar with the teaching in Scripture that to follow Jesus involves dying to ourselves, "Those who find their life will lose it, and those who lose their life for my sake will find it."[13] In effect, it is certainly a challenge to reconcile the practice of following God's will with the way we exercise our free will on a daily basis.

Some resolution to this dilemma can be reached by the language we use in understanding how God's will or action as it is presented to us. For example, author and retreat leader Mary Sharon Moore offers a positive spin on this issue by seeing God's will as an *invitation*:

> The question, "Might you have an invitation for me," communicates to me as much as to the Lord that I am available, open to divine possibility, quite agreeable, even, to what God might have in mind, even though I may have no idea right now what these words mean.[14]

In this way, our consent becomes an openness, readiness, and responsiveness to this invitation. In a similar vein, Evelyn Underhill speaks of the spiritual life as one of *cooperation with God*. She teaches that it is not so much that our will is buried; rather, it is that we try to align our will with God's will. In this way, there is a *oneness* between God's will and our will—God's action is carried out in the world through our *cooperation*. In her words:

---

13. Matt 10:39.
14. Moore, *Lord, Teach Us to Pray*, 92.

Section Three: Building the Temple

Cooperation. What does that mean? It means we shall not live up to our call as spiritual creatures unless we are willing to pull our weight. The theological axiom that "Man's will and God's grace rise and fall together" must be translated into practical terms, and given practical effect . . . we form part of the creative apparatus of God.[15]

Underhill clarifies for us that we not only cooperate with God's will for our sake, but in doing so, we are helping to enact God's action in the world. Similarly, at the Second Vatican Council in Rome on renewal in the Catholic church, our instrumental role in carrying out God's work was succinctly and profoundly proclaimed in the *Pastoral Constitution of the Church in the Modern World*: "Christ is now at work in the hearts of men through the energy of His Holy Spirit."[16]

I find it helpful to look beyond my own needs regarding free will, to what prominent spiritual writer Richard Rohr calls the "bigger life."[17] This concept helps me to realize I am being offered an extraordinary invitation, an astonishing grace really, to be one of God's instruments for helping God's action to be delivered in the world. The challenge for me is to dedicate my will to be open, receptive, and responsive to God's action however and whenever it may be manifested. Clearly, this requires a leap in faith and a deep trust in God's grace for this privilege of participating in God's action in this way.

Consenting to God's Will in a Busy Life

Many Christians would say, and rightfully so, that they live very busy lives and are daily challenged with multiple demands from raising a family, making a living (and in many cases working more than one job to make ends meet), dealing with health issues, taking care of elderly family members, the challenges we face through COVID-19, and so on. The question arises: "How on earth can we

---

15. Underhill, *Spiritual Life*, 83–84.
16. Pope Paul VI, *Gaudium et Spes*, #38 para.2.
17. Rohr, "True Self/Separate Self," para.4.

Contemplative Prayer

create space to do God's will?" Even when we try to create space, we sense that we are too preoccupied, or distracted, to become aware of God's will for us.

The answer to this question, trying to do God's will in the context of very busy lives, lies with our thinking. No, it is not that we are too busy. Rather, it is the thinking that God's will is something *outside of our daily living—something to be squeezed in.* We are in need of some new learning. That is, with the proper intention, these very responsibilities we engage in on a daily basis can be seen as God's will for us. It is not that we are too busy to pray. Rather, the very duties that keep us busy, when turned over to God, become prayer. Our challenge, our invitation, is to live each moment in the presence of God, to dedicate all we do to God, and allow God's grace to flow through these events in our daily lives. In this way we become our true selves. Thomas Merton uses the metaphor of a tree to teach us that in being our true selves, what we are created for, we are consenting to God's will:

> A tree gives glory to God by being a tree. For in being what God means it to be it is obeying God. It "consents," so to speak, to God's creative love. It is expressing an idea which is in God and which is not distinct from the essence of God, and therefore a tree imitates God by being a tree.[18]

Once we realize that all we do, with the right intention, can become wonderfully rich avenues for consenting to God's will, as Merton goes on to say, "Every moment and every event of every man's life on earth plants something in his soul."[19] In other words, these daily events and responsibilities that we may deem "busy busy," can be *transformed* into God's loving action.

Our response to God's action in this way lies with our *intention*. We need to constantly offer and dedicate all we do each day to God. It was noted in chapter 6 that a critical step at the beginning stage of our meditation is to pay particular attention to expressing your intention. That is, we not only express our intention to

18. Merton, *New Seeds of Contemplation*, 29.
19. Merton, *New Seeds of Contemplation*, 75.

Section Three: Building the Temple

rest in God's presence and action during the meditation, but also throughout the day. One helpful strategy for developing a seamless transition between our meditation period and engaging in the rest of our day is to use a sacred word or phrase. It was also mentioned in chapter 6 that practitioners of centering prayer (a form of contemplative prayer) make use of a sacred word or phrase to express their intention at the beginning of their meditation period. This sacred word or phrase can also be used throughout the day to provide constant reminders of the presence of God in all we do, and to buttress against activities that may be detrimental to God's action with and through us.

Responding to God's Call— Participating in God's Action

While God's action can be manifested through all the activities we engage in during the day, there is another way—through *specific calls* from God. That is, we may be called upon or invited to undertake a particular action. There are a number of ways in which we may experience being drawn to some particular action, that through the eyes of faith can be seen as opportunities for consenting to God's action—doing God's will.

Call to Service

We are usually aware, at least remotely, of various organizations that provide support to people in need. Sometimes our attention may be sharply brought to bear on a particular service. This experience can come through a conversation, chance meeting with someone, public announcement, or a direct appeal from someone already involved. For example, Mary Sharon Moore describes an experience she had one morning when she was having a cup of coffee while reading the local paper. She noticed a Guest Viewpoint column describing a lunchtime mentor program for middle-school students. The program involved matching a student who struggled with reading with an adult. The idea was that the adult would listen to the student read in a one-to-one situation and provide encouragement and support as needed. She said that, "In reading the Guest Viewpoint, and all through the training, something within me instinctively responds to the invitation—*Come!*"[20] In effect, she felt called to undertake this service for these children struggling with their reading at school.

There may be many opportunities throughout our lives where we experience an inward tug to offer our help, or utilize our gifts, and to support others in need. In this way, through the eyes of faith, we are consenting to God's action in the world.

Changing a Harmful Habit—Moment of Clarity

Another way we may be called to follow God's will is to address a habit we have that is harmful to ourselves and others. For example, in a book I co-authored with Bob Wiese and Tina Wells on dealing with alcoholism, we describe a moment of clarity:

> This moment, sometimes called an "aha" moment, occurs when the alcoholic becomes acutely aware of the repercussions following the last bout of drinking. It may be the individual sees very clearly the effects drinking have on self, one's career, or health, and on others . . . In effect the individual has a sudden realization that big changes need to occur.[21]

This moment of clarity can serve as a first step in recovery given the individual is willing to undertake the necessary follow-up steps. Again, through the eyes of faith, the individual can see this moment of clarity as a calling to follow God's will in becoming sober and living a fuller and richer life.

---

20. Moore, *Dare to Believe*, 86–87.
21. Colvin et al., *Break the Cycle of Alcoholism*, 35–36.

Section Three: Building the Temple

Addressing Annoying Faults

Most of us would agree we are not perfect and we have faults and failings that bother other people, such as: not picking up our clothes and goods in the living room; not taking more turns with cooking and doing the dishes; not being more thoughtful of others; not displaying kindness at work in troublesome situations; not managing outbursts of anger; and not letting go of of resentments. Sometimes we experience a moment of clarity where it becomes clear to us that a certain established behavior of ours negatively affects others and that we should make a change. When we respond to this heightened awareness and make changes that remove or lessen aggravation for others, with trust in God, we are more fully consenting to God's action in our world.

Reaching Out to Someone in Need

How often in our lifetime have we come across situations when we sense someone we know is hurting for one reason or another. We see they are struggling and we may or may not know what is causing the person to be stressed. We also have this uncomfortable dilemma of wanting to extend the hand of friendship in support and compassion but don't want to appear intrusive or nosy with something that may be personal. In similar situations, we may feel the need to apologize to someone or to take the blame for a problem but we are hesitant because the person may not accept our overtures or may even react negatively. These cases of reaching out to someone when we are uncertain of the outcome can be seen as God's action through us. God may be supporting this person through my reaching out. Granted, it is a risk to reach out in these situations, but when we trust in God, and realize that we are responding to a call from God to reach out to this person we cannot go wrong. Author and Professor of Religious Studies William Apel reminds us, "It is not what we do but what God does in us."[22] It comes down to having the intention to be an instrument in

---

22. Apel, *Silent Conversations*, 121.

Contemplative Prayer

bringing God's grace and support to this person—in reaching out we are consenting to God's action in the world.

Taking a Stand

It is safe to say that everyone, at some time or another, will face a situation where they feel called to take a stand. For example, when one senses a need to speak up in the face of some injustice that is occurring in the work force, in the community, or at national and global levels. Typically, in the context of consenting of God's action, there are two questions that should be addressed when taking a stand: First, is the issue something that is contrary to Christian beliefs that are centered on the teachings of Jesus? Second, is the action taken consistent with Christian practices?

America, for example, is presently facing a nationwide crisis concerning police brutality toward Blacks. People across the nation have responded in many different ways to the ongoing killing of Blacks by police in highly questionable circumstances. There is an unending issue of justice and accountability. Clearly, justice, individual rights, and fair treatment for all, are Christian values we must honor and live by. In addition, the way we take a stand must also be in keeping with Christian values. The burning and destruction of property, looting, fighting and brawling, and putting people in harm's way are not compatible with Christian teachings. However, participating in peaceful marches, writing letters to newspapers and government officials, lobbying at government levels, challenging officials, and, above all, supporting coordinated efforts to bring about change, are not only lawful procedures but are obligations we must pursue in our spiritual pathway.

In my own case, I find I am more and more being drawn to this issue of justice for people of color, and in particular to the Black Lives Matter movement. I sense I need to take a stronger stand here. It strikes me that I first need to listen more closely to what Blacks are saying, and to do this I have committed to undertake more reading of Black literature that has included the works

Section Three: Building the Temple

of Isabel Wilkerson,[23] Eddie Glaude Jr.,[24] James Baldwin,[25] Peniel Joseph,[26] and Kim Johnson.[27] Also, to my knowledge, there are no Black members of the Christian church I belong to, or Black participants in the groups where I meditate. I am feeling a need to worship and pray with a community that has more diversity, particularly one where Black members are present. Finally, I am unsure at this stage as to what I need to engage in to actively support Black movements to bring about change. I plan to explore avenues that may be a good fit for my involvement so that I can make a stand.

In general, there are many opportunities throughout our daily lives to consent to God's action in the world. The challenge for us is to be open, receptive, and responsive to God's action as it appears to us in these different ways. At the start of our meditation each day we are reminded to express our intention to rest in the presence of God during the meditation, but also to be ready and willing to cooperate with God's action throughout the rest of the day as well.

Discerning God's Will

While it is somewhat easy to put down on paper what it means to consent to God's action, it is ever so much more difficult to put it into practice—to connect with reality. One reason is that we are often troubled by wondering if we are following God's will or our own will. Am I deluding myself into thinking some action I undertake is God's will when, in reality, I am doing it for my own purposes? Or, is my true self operating or my false self? In some cases, we strongly sense that we need to take action on a problem, and find there are several ways for remedying the situation. Which

---

23. Wilkerson, *Caste*.
24. Glaude, *Begin Again*.
25. Baldwin, *James Baldwin*.
26. Joseph, *Sword and the Shield*.
27. Johnson, *This Is My America*

approach do I take? Or, I may be in a situation that calls for substantial changes in my life, such as: the need to relocate, change my job, let people go in my business, or make a long-term decision concerning family members. What decision do I make? Moreover, some decisions involve trade-offs. That is, the decision may benefit some people and cause problems for others. Or, the decision may cause short-term problems but will solve the problems in the long term. There are some spiritual practices that can be helpful in clarifying God's will in these challenging situations.

Spiritual Discernment

A Christian approach to addressing these situations of uncertainty that have significant ramifications is broadly called *spiritual discernment*. In effect, we prayerfully examine the pros and cons of the choices while expressing the intention of wanting to consent to God's will—to trust in God's action. Henri Nouwen describes spiritual discernment in this way:

> Discernment is a spiritual understanding and an experiential knowledge of how God is active in daily life that is acquired through disciplined spiritual practice. Discernment is faithful living and listening to God's love and direction so that we can fulfill our individual calling and shared mission.[28]

Spiritual Direction

Another way to find help in discerning God's will in difficult situations is to take part in the practice of *spiritual direction*. Simply put, spiritual direction involves conversation with another person who allows you to explore your options, weigh the choices, review events, address your ups and downs, identify possible outcomes, and examine recommendations. The spiritual director is typically trained and often is viewed as a teacher.

28. Nouwen, *Discernment*, 3.

Section Three: Building the Temple

Some practitioners find spiritual direction through a more informal association such as communicating regularly with a friend, a spiritual companion, or a soul mate. In this way, a person may find clarification concerning ways of consenting to God's will through these conversations.

Daily Examen

Throughout the ages Christians have had the practice of a *daily examen*, where one is encouraged to review events of the day in terms of fidelity to one's spiritual pathway. This practice enables one to reflect on the active presence of God over the course of a day, express gratitude for God's blessings, identify where we have been unmindful or neglectful, and humbly ask for God's action and grace for renewed resolve in the coming day. It is also helpful to include this intention at the start of the next meditation session.

Living with Uncertainty

It is very important to understand that even though we follow several steps to discern God's will for us with the best of intentions, we still may have doubts and some confusion regarding the decisions we make. While we wish it were otherwise, things never seem to be black-and-white. There often seems to be an element of risk and uncertainty. This confusion and challenge can simply arise from the basic belief that we have *free will* to begin with and that aligning our will with that of God is no simple matter. In fact, this confusion is probably a necessary part of the process of letting go of our own will and trusting in the will of God. Thomas Merton underscored these thoughts and feelings so fully and humbly when he wrote:

> My Lord God, I have no idea where I am going. I do not see the road ahead of me. I cannot know for certain where it will end . . . Therefore, will I trust you always though I may seem to be lost and in the shadow of death.

Contemplative Prayer

I will not fear, for you are ever with me, and will never leave me to face my perils alone.[29]

In sum, the spiritual practice of consenting to God's action must be seen first of all as a gratuitous gift from God, a grace in which we are shown how God continually speaks to us at all levels, whether deep in our hearts and feelings, in events of the day, in joys and sorrows, in our decisions, in experiences in nature and the arts, and so on. Second, in consenting to God's will we are serving as an instrument for God's action not just for ourselves but, more importantly, for God's people. In effect, we are consenting and committing to a spiritual pathway where we are invited to say, "In God we live and move and have our being."[30]

For Personal Application

1. Do any of the writings from Scripture or spiritual leaders resonate with you?
2. How do you reconcile doing God's will with having your own will?
3. What is the status in your practice of seeing God's will in your daily responsibilities?
4. In what ways have you experienced God's call in your life?
5. How do you try to discern God's will in the events of your life?

> **Action Response**: Is there something *specific* this chapter that draws you to make a change in, or add to, your spiritual journey?

---

29. Merton, *Thoughts in Solitude*, 79.
30. Acts 17:28.

Closing Remarks

The most powerful prayer, one well-nigh omnipotent, and the worthiest work of all is the outcome of a quiet mind. The quieter the mind, the more powerful, the worthier, the deeper, the more telling and more perfect the prayer is . . . A quiet mind is one which nothing weighs on, nothing worries, which, free from ties and from all self-seeking, is wholly merged into the will of God and dead to its own.[1]

—MEISTER ECKHART

THIS BOOK WAS WRITTEN to meet a need not only for myself, but also for others who may be experiencing a void in their prayer life or who are not quite satisfied with their practice. The primary concern, for me at least, was that current Christian church services and practices, as experienced, became routine, and motivation to participate began to wane. I began a search by attending services at churches from different Christian denominations, as well as some temples and centers with Eastern affiliations, including Buddhism and Hinduism. I found I was strongly drawn to the practice of meditation and joined a local Buddhist temple where meditation (zazen) was widely practiced. It became very clear to me that meditation needs to be a central practice in my prayer life. After a little over three years, I began to realize I needed a Christ-centered approach to meditation—with the divine indwelling becoming

1. Eckhart, *Pocket Meister Eckhart*, 15.

Closing Remarks

the focus of my meditation. I then located a Christian church that highlighted contemplative prayer in their services. I now have the opportunity to participate in traditional church services (my roots) and also to incorporate a meditation practice. I believe I have found my spiritual home.

At this time also, I began to talk to and informally interview several people who have undertaken meditation in one form or another. My intent was to get a sense of what holds people to their meditation practice and what presents challenges and difficulties. My findings were presented in a recent article published in *Episcopal Café Magazine* titled "Christian Meditation: A Gift from God." While the article was reasonably well received, the most common feedback was that it didn't go far enough. This book is my attempt to examine the subject of meditation in more depth with the particular focus of developing a sustainable practice of contemplative prayer for the laity.

It soon became clear that there are many forms of meditation which, of course, indicates there is quite a range in preferred practices. In this book, one particular form of meditation is examined—*contemplative prayer*. Specifically, contemplative prayer is presented as a prayer form with a twofold focus: *resting in God's presence* and *consenting to God's action*. For many of us, the practice of prayer from our early days as children to involvement with church services as adults has involved the utterance of words in many ways, accompanied by considerable movement. So, it becomes particularly challenging for the practitioner, with this grounding of prayer linked to words and movement, to engage in a prayer form that centers on *stillness* and *silence*.

Another challenge to a contemplative prayer practice is tied to our understanding of God. Again, most of us have a history of seeing God as a separate being from ourselves, a superior being "somewhere out there." However, a fundamental belief, a pillar of contemplative prayer, is that God dwells within us at the very core of our being—*the divine indwelling*. Our contemplative prayer practice then becomes a response to God's call to oneness with God at the center of our being and in the multiple events of our day.

Closing Remarks

One of the pitfalls from our prayer life being so dependent on our words and actions is that we become conditioned to think prayer is dependent solely on our efforts. We, or someone on our behalf, are voicing words and engaging in self-directed activities, which means we think we are in control of prayer. By contrast, contemplative prayer rests on the belief that prayer is a *gift from God*. This means we must constantly remind ourselves that our efforts do not make prayer happen. Rather, our efforts are designed to *dispose* ourselves to be open, receptive, and responsive to this extraordinary gift of God's presence and action at the center of our being.

While contemplative prayer does pose new and significant challenges to everyday Christians, we find strong encouragement, helpful information, and guidance from Scripture, and the lives of the saints, spiritual authors, retreat leaders, and practitioners. One particularly important area for establishing and sustaining a practice is to pay careful attention to the set-up details, *the logistics*. Practitioners strongly recommend that individuals check out what details work best for them and be vigilant in consistently implementing them.

Perhaps the biggest challenge for the contemplative prayer practitioner is to garner some understanding of the twofold essence of contemplative prayer—*resting in God's presence* and *consenting to God's action*. Moreover, we need to expand our concept of prayer from not only to what happens during the contemplative prayer session, but also to what happens during the course of the day. Thomas Merton captures the mystery of contemplative prayer and the underlying need to trust in God's beneficence when he writes:

> I do not think contemplation can be taught, but certainly an aptitude for it can be awakened. It is an aptitude which quite a lot of people might have, in seminaries and monasteries at least, as well as in any walk of life. . . . Simply be content to let God use you in whatever way He wills, and be sure you do not get in His way with misplaced initiatives.[2]

2. Merton, "Letter to Etta Gullick," 179.

Closing Remarks

In closing, contemplative prayer—resting in God's presence and consenting to God's action—is a challenging and rewarding way to pray. There is no sense that it is the only way to pray, nor the best way. Rather, it is an approach, with God's grace, that can be a rewarding part of our spiritual journey—a wondrous gift from God.

Bibliography

Alban Institute. "Silence." https://alban.org/archive/silence/.
Anonymous Author. *The Cloud of Unknowing & The Book of Privy Counseling.* Edited by William Johnston. New York: Doubleday, 1996.
———. *The Cloud of Unknowing with the Book of Privy Counsel.* Translated by Carmen Acevedo Butcher. Boston: Shambhala, 2009.
Apel, William. *Silent Conversations: Reading the Bible in Good Company.* Valley Forge, PA: Judson, 2000.
Armstrong, Karen. *The Case for God.* New York: Knopf, 2009.
Baldwin, James. *James Baldwin: The Complete Works.* Hawthorne, CA: BN, 1972.
Bonhoeffer, Dietrich. *Letters and Papers from Prison.* New York: MacMillan, 1967.
Borg, Marcus. *The God We Never Knew: Beyond Dogmatic Religion to a More Authentic Contemporary Faith.* San Francisco: HarperSanFrancisco, 1997.
Bourgeault, Cynthia. *Centering Prayer and Inner Awakening.* Lanham, MD: Cowley, 2004.
———. *The Heart of Centering Prayer: Nondual Christianity in Theory and Practice.* Boulder, CO: Shambhala, 2016.
———. "The Method." *Center for Action and Contemplation*, February 13, 2017. https://cac.org/the-method-2017-02-13/.
———. *Mystical Hope: Trusting in the Mercy of God.* Cambridge, MA: Cowley, 2001.
Braza, Jerry. *Practicing Mindfulness: Finding Calm and Focus in Your Everyday Life.* North Clarendon, VT: Tuttle, 2020.
Bruteau, Beatrice. *Radical Optimism: Practical Spirituality in an Uncertain World.* Boulder, CO: Sentient, 2002.
———. *What We Can Learn from the East.* New York: Crossroad, 1995.
Casey, Michael. *Grace: On the Journey to God.* Brewster, MA: Paraclete, 2018.
———. *Toward God: The Ancient Wisdom of Western Prayer.* Ligouri, MO: Ligouri, 1996.
Caussade, Jean-Pierre de. *Abandonment to Divine Providence.* New York: Doubleday, 1975.

Bibliography

Chardin, Teilhard de. *The Divine Milieu*. New York: Harper Perennial, 1960.
Colvin, Geoff. "Christian Meditation: A Gift from God." *Episcopal Café Magazine*, April 18, 2020. https://www.episcopalcafe.com/christian-meditation-a-gift-from-god/.
Colvin, Geoff, and Pat Foley. *Living with Paradoxes: A Spiritual Approach*. Eugene, OR: Behavior Associates, 2019.
Colvin, Geoff, et al. *Break the Cycle of Alcoholism: Skills for Healthy Sobriety*. Eugene, OR: Behavior Associates, 2012.
Cyzewski, Ed. "Flee, Be Silent, Pray Quotes." https://www.goodreads.com/work/quotes/56623726-flee-be-silent-pray.
Day, Dorothy. *The Reckless Way of Love: Notes on Following Jesus*. Walden, NY: Plough, 2017.
Eckhart, Meister. *The Complete Mystical Works of Meister Eckhart*. Translated by Maurice O'C Walshe. New York: Crossroad, 2009.
———. *The Pocket Meister Eckhart*. Edited by David O'Neal. Boulder, CO: Shambhala, 2018.
Epictetus. *Manual for Living*. Interpreted by Sharon Lebell. New York: HarperCollins, 1994.
Finley, James. *Christian Meditation: Experiencing the Presence of God*. New York: HarperOne, 2004.
Forem, Jack. *Transcendental Meditation: A Manual for Christian Meditation*. 2nd ed. Carlsbad, CA: Hay House, 2012.
Gallagher, Timothy. *Meditation and Contemplation: An Ignatian Guide to Praying with Scripture*. Chestnut Ridge, NY: Crossroad, 2008.
Glaude, Eddie S., Jr. *Begin Again: James Baldwin's America and Its Urgent Lessons for Our Own*. New York: Crown, 2020.
Haase, Albert. *Coming Home to Your True Self: Leaving the Emptiness of False Attractions*. Downer's Grove, IL: InterVarsity, 2008.
Heraclitus. *Fragments: The Collected Wisdom of Heraclitus*. Translated by Brooks Haxton. New York: Viking Penguin, 2001.
Heuertz, Phileena. *Mindful Silence: The Heart of Christian Contemplation*. Downers Grove, IL: InterVarsity, 2018.
Hillesum, Etty. *An Interrupted Life: The Diaries, 1941–1943, and Letters from Westerbrook*. Translated by Arnold J. Pomerans. New York: Holt, 1996.
Hopkins, Gerard Manley. "God's Grandeur." In *The Poems of Gerard Manley Hopkins*, edited by William H. Gardner and Norman H. MacKenzie, 66. 4th ed. Oxford: Oxford University Press, 1967.
Jager, Willigis. *Contemplation: A Christian Path*. Liguori, MO: Triumph, 1994.
Jalics, Franz. *The Contemplative Way: Quietly Savoring God's Presence*. New York: Paulist, 2011.
Johnson, Kim. *This Is My America*. New York: Random House, 2020.
Johnston, William. *The Mysticism of the Cloud of Unknowing*. New York: Fordham University Press, 2000.
Joseph, Peniel E. *The Sword and the Shield: The Revolutionary Lives of Malcolm X and Martin Luther King Jr.* New York: Basic, 2020.

Bibliography

Julian of Norwich. *Revelation of Love.* New York: Image, 1996.
Kabat-Zinn. *Mindfulness for Beginners: Reclaiming the Present Moment—And Your Life.* Boulder, CO: Sounds True, 2012.
Keating, Thomas. *Consenting to God as God Is.* New York: Lantern, 2016.
———. *The Mystery of Christ: The Liturgy as Spiritual Experience.* New York: Continuum, 2008.
———. *Open Mind, Open Heart.* 20th Anniversary Ed. New York: Continuum, 2006.
Knitter, Paul F. *Without Buddha I Could Not Be a Christian.* Oxford: Oneworld, 2009.
Kornfield, Jack. "Letting Go." https://jackkornfield.com/letting-go/.
Laird, Martin. *Into the Silent Land: A Guide to the Christian Practice of Contemplation.* New York: Oxford University Press, 2006.
Larkin, Ernest E. "Contemplative Prayer as the Soul of the Apostolate." http://carmelnet.org/larkin/larkin020.pdf.
Main, John. *Words into Silence: A Manual for Christian Meditation.* Norwich, UK: Canterbury, 2006.
Matthiesson, Peter. *The Snow Leopard.* New York: Viking, 1978.
McColman, Carl. *Answering the Contemplative Call: First Steps on the Mystical Path.* Charlottsville, VA: Hampton Roads, 2013.
Merton, Thomas. *The Ascent to Truth.* New York: Harvest, 1951.
———. *The Asian Journal of Thomas Merton.* New York: New Directions, 1975.
———. *The Climate of Monastic Prayer.* Collegeville, MN: Liturgical, 2018.
———. *Conjectures of a Guilty Bystander.* New York: Doubleday, 1965.
———. *Contemplative Prayer.* New York: Image, 1969.
———. *Day of a Stranger.* Salt Lake City: Gibbs M. Smith, 1981.
———. *Dialogues with Silence: Prayers and Drawings.* Edited by Jonathon Montaldo. New York: HarperCollins, 2001.
———. *Hidden in the Same Mystery: Thomas Merton and Loretto.* Edited by Bonnie Thurston, et al. Louisville, KY: Fons Vitae, 2010.
———. "Letter to Abdul Haziz, 2 January 1966." In *The Hidden Ground of Love: The Letters of Thomas Merton on Religious Experience and Social Concerns,* edited by William H. Shannon, 43–67. New York: Farrar, Straus and Giroux, 1985.
———. "Letter to Daisetz T. Suzuki, April 11, 1959." In *Thomas Merton: A Life in Letters: The Essential Collection,* edited by William H. Shannon and Christine M. Bochen, 358–65. New York: HarperOne, 2008.
———. "Letter to Etta Gullick." In *Thomas Merton: A Life in Letters,* edited by William Shannon and Christine Bochen, 170–82. New York: HarperOne, 2008.
———. *New Seeds of Contemplation.* New York: New Directions, 1961.
———. *Seasons of Celebration.* New York: Farrar, Straus and Giroux, 1965.
———. *Seeds of Contemplation.* London: Hollis & Carter, 1949.
———. *The Springs of Contemplation: A Retreat at the Abbey of Gethsemani.* New York: Farrar, Straus and Giroux, 1992.

Bibliography

———. *Thoughts in Solitude*. New York: Farrar, Straus and Giroux, 1978.
Milone, L. J. *Nothing but God: The Everyday Mysticism of Meister Eckhart*. Eugene, OR: Resource, 2019.
Moore, Mary Sharon. *Dare to Believe: Rise Up to Act*. Eugene, OR: Awakening Vocations, 2019.
———. *Lord, Teach Us to Pray: An Intimate Look into a Maturing Prayer Life*. Eugene, OR: Awakening Vocations, 2017.
Myss, Caroline. *Entering the Castle: An Inner Path to God and Your Soul*. New York: Free Press, 2007.
Nhat Hanh, Thich. *Your True Home: The Everyday Wisdom of Thich Nhat Hanh: 365 Days of Practical, Powerful Teachings from the Beloved Zen Teacher*. Boulder, CO: Shambhala, 2011.
Nouwen, Henri. *Discernment: Reading the Signs of Daily Life*. New York: HarperOne, 2013.
———. "Let Yourself Be Useless." https://henrinouwen.org/meditation/let-yourself-be-useless/.
———. *The Path of Waiting*. New York: Crossroad, 1995.
O'Connor, Elizabeth. *Journey Inward, Journey Outward*. New York: HarperCollins, 1975.
O'Donohue, John. *Anam Cara: A Book of Celtic Wisdom*. New York: Harper Perennial, 1997.
Ozeki, Ruth. *A Tale for the Time Being*. New York: Viking, 2013.
Paintner, Christine Valters. *Lectio Divina: Transforming Words & Images into Heart-Centered Prayer*. Woodstock, VT: Skylight Paths, 2011.
Pope, Alexander. *An Essay on Criticism*. http://www.gutenberg.org/cache/epub/7409/pg7409.txt.
Pope Paul VI. *Gaudium et Spes*. http://www.vatican.va/archive/hist_councils/ii_vatican_council/documents/vat-ii_const_19651207_gaudium-et-spes_en.html.
Prochnik, George. *In Pursuit of Silence: Listening for Meaning in a World of Noise*. New York: Anchor, 2010.
Rahner, Karl. *The Need and the Blessing of Prayer*. Translated by Bruce W. Gillette. Collegeville, MN: Liturgical, 1997.
Rohr, Richard. *A Spring within Us: A Book of Daily Reflections*. Albuquerque, NM: CAC, 2016.
———. "True Self/Separate Self." *Center for Action and Contemplation*, August 30, 2020. https://cac.org/true-self-separate-self-2020-08-30.
Shannon, William H., et al. *The Thomas Merton Encyclopedia*. Maryknoll, NY: Orbis, 2002.
Stella, Tom. *The God Instinct: Heeding Your Heart's Unrest*. Notre Dame, IN: Sorin, 2001.
St. John of the Cross. *The Dark Night of the Soul*. http://www.carmelitemonks.org/Vocation/DarkNight-StJohnoftheCross.pdf.
St. Mother Teresa of Calcutta. "How They Prayed." In *Stories of Encounter* by Roddy Hamilton, 162–64. Edinburgh: Saint Andrews, 2017.

Bibliography

St. Richard of Chichester. "Acts and Other Devotions." In *The Churchman's Prayer Manual*, compiled by G. R. Bullock-Webster, 21–34. 3rd ed. London: n.p., 1913. https://archive.org/stream/churchmansprayeroobulluoft/mode/2up.

St. Teresa of Avila. "Chapter 28." https://www.ecatholic2000.com/stteresa/way35.shtml.

Suzuki, Shunryru. *Zen Mind, Beginner's Mind*. New York: Weatherhill, 1970.

Taylor, Brian. *Becoming Christ: Transformation through Contemplation*. Cambridge, MA: Cowley, 2002.

Thurman, Howard. *With Head and Heart: The Autobiography of Howard Thurman*. Orlando: Harcourt Brace, 1979.

Thurston, Bonnie, and Sr. Mary Swain, eds. *Hidden in the Same Mystery: Thomas Merton and Loretto*. Louisville, KY: Fons Vitae, 2010.

Tolle, Eckhart. *Essential Meditations with Eckhart Tolle: Guided Sessions and Practical Teachings*. Audio CD. Louisville, CO: Sounds True, 2020.

Underhill, Evelyn. *The Spiritual Life: Four Broadcast Talks*. Mansfield Centre, CT: Martino, 2013.

Ware, Kallistos. *The Inner Kingdom: Volume 1 of the Collected Works*. 6 vols. Crestwood, NY: St. Vladamir's Seminary, 2004.

Weil, Simone. *Gravity and Grace*. Abingdon-on-Thames, UK: Routledge Classics, 2002.

———. *Love in the Void: Where God Finds Us*. Walden, NY: Plough, 2018.

———. *Waiting for God*. New York: Harper Perennial Modern Classics, 2009.

Wiesel, Elie. *Night*. New York: Hill and Wang, 1958.

Wilkerson, Isabel. *Caste: The Origins of Our Disconents*. New York: Random House, 2020.

www.ingramcontent.com/pod-product-compliance
Lightning Source LLC
Chambersburg PA
CBHW070455100426
42743CB00010B/1628